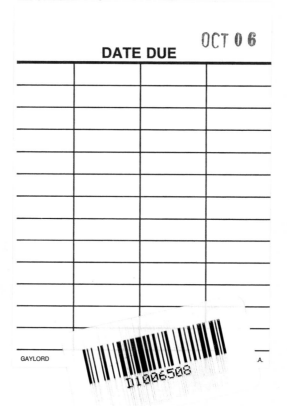

Donated by
Anthony E. Ramsey M.D.

JACKSON COUNTY
Library Services

The Secret of
HOGAN'S SWING

BOOKS BY PRINTER BOWLER

The Cosmic Laws of Golf (and everything else)

Writing Naturally

Spirit of Montana

*Wheatflowers: Recipes for Lovers of Healthy Bodies,
Clear Minds, and Pure Hearts*

The Secret of
HOGAN'S SWING

TOM BERTRAND
with
PRINTER BOWLER

WILEY
John Wiley & Sons, Inc.

Copyright © 2006 by Tom Bertrand and Printer Bowler. All rights reserved

Published by John Wiley & Sons, Inc., Hoboken, New Jersey
Published simultaneously in Canada

Design and composition by Navta Associates, Inc.

For general information about our other products and services, please contact our Customer Care Department within the United States at (800) 762-2974, outside the United States at (317) 572-3993 or fax (317) 572-4002.

Wiley also publishes its books in a variety of electronic formats. Some content that appears in print may not be available in electronic books. For more information about Wiley products, visit our web site at www.wiley.com.

Library of Congress Cataloging-in-Publication Data

Bertrand, Tom.
　The secret of Hogan's swing / Tom Bertrand with Printer Bowler.
　　p. cm.
　ISBN-13 978-0-471-99831-0 (cloth : alk. paper)
　ISBN-10 0-471-99831-1 (cloth : alk. paper)
　1. Swing (Golf) 2. Hogan, Ben, 1912– 3. Schlee, John. I. Bowler, Printer. II. Title.
　GV979.S9B47 2005
　796.352'3—dc22

　　　　　　　　　　　　　　　　　　　　　　　　　　　　　　2006011330

Printed in the United States of America

10 9 8 7 6 5 4 3 2 1

This book is dedicated to my one and only loving God, my wife, Heidi, for her loving encouragement and unending support; my children, Logan, Lindsey, and Taylor, who lost "dad time" in the process; and our dog, Spike, my faithful writing companion.

—TB

Contents

Preface

When Tom Bertrand first called and said he wanted some help writing a golf story, I must admit I quietly groaned. In the last few years I'd written my own golf book and helped someone else write another. Enough books about golf already! I thought, as Tom started telling me what he had in mind.

When Tom mentioned that he had been a student of, and later a partner with, former Tour player John Schlee, I thought, Okay, that must have been interesting. But my antennae shot straight up when he told me that Schlee had been among the rare few to receive extensive personal instruction from the great Ben Hogan over a period of several years. Set aside the occasional tips that Hogan sparingly meted out, and you can count his serious students on one hand. Everybody wanted to learn golf from Hogan, the undisputed self-made master of the game, but you couldn't buy your way into his inner circle. You got through that door by invitation only.

Then it struck me: here I am talking to a direct link to that circle. Now I'm all ears.

Tom told me how Hogan had taught John Schlee secrets and

insights of the game that very few others, if any, knew about. John, in turn, had passed those gems of knowledge on to Tom while they worked together during the 1980s at John's Maximum Golf School.

Since then, Tom's pot of gold had simmered on the back burner while he raised a family, worked a regular job, and occasionally taught golf students the Hogan techniques he'd learned through John. Now he felt that the time and circumstances were right to set the table and invite golfers everywhere to pull up a chair and partake of his offering.

"That's the story I want you to help me tell," he said. Now I'm thinking, Maybe we just don't have enough of the *right kind* of golf books. Lately I'd been feeling that the golf world is slowly starving on a fast-food diet of tricked-up equipment and patchwork analysis. I caught the scent of a gourmet feast in what Tom was saying.

By the end of our conversation, my response had evolved from a silent groan to an audible gasp. As a golfer and a writer, I wanted to be in on this one, so I told Tom I'd do my best to help him.

I had only one condition: this should be a story, not so much for the aficionados and gurus and analysts of the game, but for average, workaday, regular people like me and the forty million other flustered floggers around the world. We're those battered souls who huff and flail away on the practice range, who read and try all the golf tips with sporadic success. We love this game for the anticipation and the thrill of finding that sweet spot, even though we're constantly befuddled and beaten up by its confounding, fickle ways. We can't afford to spend a week's take-home pay on the latest equipment fads, even though we sometimes do. We long to hear inspiring tales of our heroes and some straight scoop on the secrets of their success.

Tom heartily agreed to this condition, and off we went. As with most uncharted adventures, we didn't realize where the trail would take us until we got here. Our journey has been filled with unexpected revelations about Ben Hogan and the golf swing that set records still standing today. We also unearthed some interesting history of the game that was previously unknown to the general public. Add to that an undercurrent of Shakespearean drama driving our players onward through their turns of fortune.

In the end, I believe we've brought forward a worthwhile contribution to the lore and lustre of our favorite sport. You, of course, will be the judge of that.

So, fellow handicappers of the world, this is for you. It comes on a clean beam from the heart of the master himself straight to yours. I hope you find some useful information here to help you master the challenges of your own game. Good luck, swing smooth, and let 'er rip.

Printer Bowler

○ ○ ○

I don't know how many times I tried to complete this project over the last fifteen years, but interruptions became a way of life. Family obligations always came first, so I decided that I wouldn't start seriously teaching golf again until I was nearly fifty years of age and my children were at least half grown up.

Then about two years ago I closed down my store, Bertrand's South Jersey Deli, and an opportunity arose for my wife to be the sole breadwinner. That allowed me to work full time to chronicle a remarkable era in my life, when I was learning the secrets of Ben Hogan's legendary golf swing.

Only one problem remained: I'm not a professional writer. In fact, English was my least favorite subject in school.

I recalled the words of my former teacher and partner, the late PGA Tour player John Schlee, who once told me, "Tom, if you want something done right, you have to find a professional. If you need electrical work done, find a good electrician; if you need to sell your house, find a good real estate agent; if you need work done on your car, find a good mechanic. Don't try to do it yourself because it will only end up costing you." So, I went in search of a good writer.

I did some research on the Internet and came up with three possibilities: Curt Sampson, Bob Cullen, and Printer Bowler—all published golf book authors. I e-mailed all three and told them what I was doing. To my surprise, each responded with his phone number so that he could hear a little more.

Mr. Sampson was a delight to talk with. He asked whether I had an agent or a publisher. When I said no, he gave me advice on how to make a book proposal and even offered me his agent's phone number. Without advance money, however, he couldn't get involved.

I then talked with Mr. Cullen, and he asked the same questions: Agent? Publisher? He was nice enough but also declined due to no upfront money.

Next, I contacted Mr. Bowler. I was intrigued by the title of his book *The Cosmic Laws of Golf (and everything else)* and the fact that he had been involved with the Shivas Irons Society. That struck an interesting chord, because John Schlee used to go around saying, mostly in jest, that he was Shivas Irons.

When I phoned Mr. Bowler, he had lots of questions, but I

could tell that he had a heart of gold. He asked me to send him some of the manuscript I had written, and I knew right then that he would be the man to give me a hand, even if there was no guarantee of getting a paycheck.

That was twenty-two months ago, and I couldn't have been blessed with a better, more understanding partner than he. Printer helped to organize my piles of notes and set up a good operations plan to guide us to the finish line. He's added depth to my stories while introducing me to new levels of research. I will forever be grateful to this man because he saw a story needing to be told and was willing to go for it.

Tom Bertrand

The Secret of
HOGAN'S SWING

Introduction

In the early 1980s, I frequented a practice range at the Olympic Resort Hotel in Carlsbad, California, to tune up for the weekly skins games at Riverside and San Diego County. It was a newly conceived state-of-the-art practice facility that its creators called Olympic Golf. The idea was that you could play any course in the world right there on the range.

The facility was set up with fifty mats looking out on two 280-yard fairways. Target greens with bunkers were positioned every 25 yards out to the 225-yard mark. Small bunkers were also placed between each golfer's mat, with large chipping and putting greens located behind them.

Using a scorecard from your golf course of choice, you tee up your ball and drive it down one of the fairways. Then, based on your scorecard yardage, you hit your approach shot to the appropriate target green. If you hit near or on the green, you walk behind your mat to the practice green to chip, if necessary, and putt out the hole. If your drive lands in a fairway bunker, you step in the bunker next to your mat and proceed with your shot to the appropriate green. If your approach shot lands in a

1

greenside bunker, you step in and blast out to the practice green behind you.

It was an interesting concept and great fun, but it never caught on around the country. We local golfers felt very fortunate to have a range that lets you play a "round" of golf while you practice.

One day while I was playing a La Costa scorecard at Olympic, a stranger suddenly appeared next to my mat and barked, "That's no way to set up to a golf ball!"

Without introducing himself, he walked right up to me and, before I could say a word, grabbed my arms and shifted my body into a strained and contorted setup position. I was flabbergasted and felt like a pretzel in a straitjacket.

"Now swing at it!" he yelled, as he backed off a couple of steps.

My jammed mind was shouting at me, "Who *is* this guy and why am I letting him jump in here and do this to me?" as I started to rotate my body and club into a backswing. Then I did my best to swing at the ball and hit it dead right.

"That's all right," he said "Your body was lunging through the impact area instead of turning. Just think *turn* and your body will eventually get it." I unraveled myself, but before I could ask his name, he darted off to dump his unsolicited advice on some other unsuspecting subject.

I was a bit put off by his impromptu invasion of my space but intrigued by his quick observation of my annoying lunge. It had always been a problem, and I still hadn't solved it. I was no hack, by any means, having more than a few rounds in the 60s, but I was no touring pro either. The high point of my competitive golf had been in 1977 with a nationally ranked team at Cumberland County College in New Jersey. I was still proud of my individual second-place finish in the Junior College State Championship.

Now, despite this guy's annoying manner, I found myself wanting to hear more.

I checked around and found out he was John Schlee, a twelve-year veteran of the PGA Tour, better known as the man who finished second, one stroke behind Johnny Miller's final-round 63 in the 1973 U.S. Open at Oakmont. He had a reputation for being a talented player with a volatile and sometimes abrasive personality, whose obsession with golf left little room for anything else in his life. It was Schlee who coined the phrase "Watching Sam Snead practice is like watching fish practice swimming." And watching John Schlee give free golf advice was like watching a drill sergeant dog Marine recruits at Parris Island.

That was just the beginning. I soon discovered that John was among the very few professional golfers to have received private lessons from the great Ben Hogan over a period of several years. Unfortunately, John had had only a short time to put Hogan's priceless instruction to work on the PGA Tour. He'd been forced to give up competitive golf in 1978 when a long history of lower-back problems finally prevented him from extended practice and play.

About the time we met in 1985, John was holding three-day golf schools—nationally advertised as Maximum Golf Schools—at the Olympic Golf facility, my new stomping grounds.

A week after our first encounter, I was practicing at Olympic, when I spotted John down the line working (or interfering) with somebody hitting from the mats. Perfect, I thought. I'll just reverse our roles and barge in on *him* this time. I strolled over and caught his eye just as he was leaving another victim. In good humor but with just the right touch of impertinence, I asked, "Tell me, how often do you just walk up uninvited and start messing with other people's golf swings?"

"Hey, if they don't want to hear it, they can tell me to get lost," John replied in the same tone as my question.

Now that I'd gotten that out of my system, I smiled and introduced myself. "Hi. My name's Tom Bertrand," I said. "You came over to me last week, changed my setup, and then told me I should learn to turn instead of slide through the hitting area."

"Oh, yeah. Hi, Tom. John Schlee." He stood there for a moment with his hands on his hips, sizing me up.

Then he extended his hand, and I was surprised to see mine almost disappear into his huge paw. John stood about 6'3" and had a lean, muscular build. His large feet were accentuated by his thin frame and a pair of long legs that rose up out of his white FootJoys. He looked to be in his mid-forties. I noticed that his hair, protruding from a TaylorMade visor, was more white than gray.

"Nice to meet you," I said. "Would you mind if I ask you a few questions while you're running around out here?"

"Sure. Follow me."

So I proceeded to pick his brain for about forty-five minutes in between his heaping helpful hints on one unsuspecting golfer after another.

I had always been in search of the perfect golf swing. Since I was twelve years old, I'd read and studied everything I could get my hands on about the game of golf and the PGA Tour. So what John said next really lit me up.

After I had bombarded him with a volley of technical questions, he suddenly turned to me and said, "Why don't you come to my next golf school, and you'll learn everything you need to know about the workings of the golf swing that Ben Hogan taught me."

Wow, I thought, that would be fantastic! It would be a dream come true to sit in and hear what John had learned in person from the great Hogan. All my life, Hogan had seemed so out of reach, a distant hero I could only marvel at from afar. Now, out of the blue, a door had suddenly opened, inviting me into this renowned master's aura.

The magnitude of this opportunity had only begun to sink in when it hit me: I didn't have the $650 to put out for a session at his school. At the time I was waiting tables at a local steakhouse, earning barely enough money to make my rent and car payments. Any leftovers usually went for greens fees and golf supplies. I was enjoying a young man's seat-of-the-pants lifestyle and wasn't that interested in finding a real job, much less a career. When I heard John's invitation, though, being a broke gadabout suddenly didn't seem that glamorous. "Sorry, John. I can't," I said. "I just don't have that kind of money right now."

John smiled and said, "No, you don't have to pay me anything. Besides, I remember when I was so broke I couldn't pay attention. If you like what you see and hear, we can talk about bringing you on as an instructor at my school. I've been looking for a serious student of the game who learns fast. I like what I see, and I think you'd fit right in."

I could not believe what I was hearing. I could actually learn about Ben Hogan for free and get paid for teaching someone about the game I love? I had to pinch myself. Yes, my passion for golf could now be a part of my working life. I'd finally found my ideal job and couldn't wait to get out of bed the next day and all the days that followed.

That was the beginning of my apprenticeship and later partnership with John Schlee. When we met, he was in the midst of writing his instruction manual, soon to be published as *Maximum Golf*, and was also preparing to shoot his latest instructional video.

Thus began an enlightening and sometimes frustrating journey that would completely change my life. I would also discover the tumultuous world of John's mind that many believed to be a wide-ranging mixture of genius and absurdity in the golf teaching profession. During the next seven years, I totally dedicated myself to understanding and using the golf swing that Ben Hogan had dug out of the earth and later poured into John's thirsty mind as he had with very few others.

John was the living library where the mother lode of information was stored. I soon came to realize that the most important part of my work would be to extract, distill, and share this knowledge with the rest of the world. I felt as though fate had called me to be a chronicler of the master's wisdom, to help protect its integrity and keep it alive, to do my part in making it available to those who hunger for the real thing. I am sincerely humbled and grateful to be a part of this lineage.

In the pages that follow is my story of how Ben Hogan's monumental gifts to golf came to be accessible to everyone who loves the game. All of Hogan's secrets (including the "missing link" known only to John and a handful of others) are revealed, reviewed, and explained. Finally, after decades of analysis of and speculation about Hogan's mysterious mastery of the game, there are no more secrets.

For the first time, the complete package is available so that every golfer can comprehend and appreciate what I believe is the purest, most effective swing in the history of golf. It is my duty and pleasure to share with you these treasures.

John Schlee and Tom Bertrand in 1986

1

Meeting the Master

A Dream Comes True

He was a high-strung hotshot on the Memphis State University golf team. As tournament officials ushered him toward the Tour players' locker room, John Schlee's heart was pounding with a single thought: "I'm finally going to meet my all-time hero, Ben Hogan!" Hogan didn't play in many tournaments these days, but he was using the Memphis Invitational as a warm-up for the 1960 U.S. Open at Cherry Hills.

John's eyes darted everywhere as he strode through the corridors leading to the inner sanctum reserved exclusively for the best golfers in the world. He had never been on the inside before and didn't know what to expect. He was still reeling with awe and trepidation since he'd been told he might get this chance of a lifetime to shake hands with the legendary Ben Hogan. John's dream was to become a professional golfer, and in his young mind he believed he was about to touch the Holy Grail.

As the group approached the locker room, John picked up the acrid scent of stale cigar and cigarette smoke wafting through the humid air. His senses reveled in the complex aroma of seasoned leather, polished brass on oiled hardwood, and two kinds of sweat: one from physical exertion and the other, more acidic kind that drips from nerve endings. All melded into a rarefied atmosphere infused with victory celebrations and agonies endured by the idols of John's passion. This indeed was another world—a world he vowed he would belong to someday.

They turned a corner and there he was, cigarette lightly dangling from the left corner of his mouth. Hogan stood surrounded by reporters as he patiently parried another intrusion from the national news media. He had just posted a third-round 73 and wasn't in the best of moods.

Hogan looked more weathered and a bit shorter than John had imagined, yet the charismatic power emanating from his hero kept John standing at attention as he waited his turn. The media interview concluded a few moments later, and the official ushered John forward into Hogan's presence. Their meeting was brief, lasting barely a minute. As soon as they were introduced and shook hands, John blurted out, "I would love to learn how to play golf from you someday!"

Their eyes locked, and the room instantly fell silent. John could feel the intensity of Hogan's gaze boring straight through his eyeballs. Everyone knew that Hogan hated to give lessons.

Before Hogan had a chance to reply to this impertinent outburst, John's official escort grabbed his arm and whisked him away. The official cast an apologetic glance toward Hogan as they marched out the doorway.

○ ○ ○

John launched his professional career by earning medalist honors in the PGA Tour's first Qualifying School in the fall of 1965. He won by three strokes with an eight-round total of 583. Although he didn't win during his first year on Tour, John established himself as the new kid on the block with a run of strong showings. He finished forty-seventh on the money list and was picked as *Golf Digest*'s Rookie of the Year in 1966.

Within three years, however, his game had disintegrated in a cloud of endless tinkering and swing-tip tangents. As happens to so many who find early success, John's new confidence had spurred him on to find even greater attainment, but he was soon overwhelmed by a constant patter of free advice that cluttered his mind and left his golf swing in shambles.

Where John's plate had once been full, he was now starving to learn the truth about the golf swing, something real that would work all the time. He knew that Hogan had discovered and consistently demonstrated the keys to a pure, reliable golf swing. John pined to be his student. But how? You didn't just walk up to this legend the British labeled the "Wee Ice Mon" and ask him to save your golfing life. Yet as fate would have it, John got his chance when he needed it most.

The first time John and Hogan played golf together wasn't in a tournament or even a practice round; rather, it was a serendipitous meeting where they played eleven holes at Preston Trails in Dallas. John said it was a magical day that he would treasure for the rest of his life. Thus began the realization of his lifelong dream: to walk side by side with the master who would initiate him into a profound new understanding of the golf swing that few others would ever know.

John recalled that meeting in a story I heard a number of times in his Maximum Golf School classroom:

"One day at Preston Trails in Dallas during the spring of 1969, I was practicing at the far end of the range by myself, and along comes this golf cart. As it passes by, I notice it's Ben Hogan. I hadn't seen him since my college days at Memphis State when I made a fool of myself after being introduced to him. He drove down to the other end of the range and started hitting balls. Immediately I panicked, trying to look my best and be professional, but I was scattering golf balls everywhere.

"After what seemed like twenty minutes, he drove his cart back toward me, stopped, and said, 'John, would you like to play?' I didn't think he would even remember my name, let alone invite me to join him. I couldn't put my clubs in his cart fast enough.

"We drove over to the first hole, grabbed our drivers, and proceeded to the tee box. He turned to me and wanted to know if we should wager a little something. I started digging in my pockets to see if I had any money to lose, and I found $22. Ben said that would do.

"Ben teed his ball and ripped it down the right-center of the fairway about 275 yards. I got up and hooked my drive into the thick rough about 265 yards out. After we finished the first hole, we both had pars, one miraculous and one routine. I dropped a 65-foot downhill double-breaker that found the center of the cup, while Ben two-putted from 9 feet. He didn't say a word.

"Actually, he didn't say a word until we finished the fifth hole. At that point, I was one under, having used only five putts in five holes. I was making them from everywhere. Ben was one over with eleven putts. On the fifth, I holed a par putt from about 45 feet, and Ben three-putted from less than 15. He snatched his ball out of the cup and exploded.

"He glared at me and said I was ruining everything he had

worked his whole life to create. He told me that I was confused and had no idea how to swing a golf club—all I could do was putt. He was absolutely right, but I had just made a par to go two up on this legendary figure, and I couldn't resist a comment after his rant.

"'Does this mean you don't want to press?' I heard myself saying. I could almost see the steam escaping from his ears.

"He looked at me for a few seconds, then smiled and slowly shook his head. I knew he was thinking, 'What am I going to do with this weirdo?' But he sensed my passion for the game and knew I truly wanted to learn how to hit a golf ball properly. So, over the next few holes, we continued what was to become my eye-opening journey into Ben Hogan's world of golf.

"Oh, yes—Hogan didn't press, and I was still two-up when we stopped playing after the eleventh hole. He never offered to pay me the $22 bet, and I was so star-struck playing golf with him that I forgot all about it."

The Teacher and the Student

In the fall of 1969, John and Ben started getting together at Shady Oaks Country Club in Fort Worth, Texas. They met on a regular basis over the next five years, usually there on Hogan's home turf.

In those days, John was still playing on the Tour and traveling out of his home base in Brownsville. He was on the road for two or three weeks at a time, then often dropped by Shaky Oaks with a handful of notes he'd written on stationery from various motels. John was meticulous in tracking his swing performance and the results of each golf shot. After each tournament round, he went back to his motel room and jotted down a list of things he wanted to go over with Hogan.

At first, John focused mainly on remedying his weak points, and by 1969, there were many. He soon found, however, that Hogan was not that concerned with solving "swing problems." Hogan's sole interest was in creating and maintaining an effective, repeatable golf swing. Thus, they would simply abandon the techniques and thought patterns governing John's current swing and build a completely new one from scratch.

During one of their first meetings, Hogan went into detail about establishing a proper grip with both hands set in a "weak" position (left thumb on top of shaft, palms facing). John said that the first time he tried this new grip was a disaster. He hit a driver, and the ball sailed 270 yards dead right, over homes walled with plate-glass windows. Hogan did everything he could not to burst out laughing.

The so-called weak grip was a novelty even in 1969. Many touring professionals back in the fifties and sixties, including John, were "handsy" players. They used a strong left-hand grip, slid their bodies into the impact area, hit against a firm left side, and squared up the clubface by flipping their hands at the last possible second. If they flipped them too early, they would hook the shot. If they flipped too late, they would slice or push it right.

Because of the hand position Hogan prescribed for the grip, John said he couldn't manipulate his hands to close the clubface on the downswing. He would have to change everything now, and this strange new grip was only the beginning.

Hogan wanted John to train the bigger muscles of his body to do the work that his hands had been assigned all along. The hips and the torso must turn around the spine, like a swinging door fixed on its hinges, and power the movement of arms and hands through the ball. When the bigger muscles learn their assignment and the hands become more passive, Hogan said, the swing will become stronger and far more reliable. Before Hogan's time, these movements were virtually unheard of and were considered revolutionary by the few who were aware of them.

As strange as it was for John during the early days of his transformation, he couldn't argue with the validity of Hogan's seemingly radical approach. The career said it all: 9 major championships and 54 other wins, with 241 top-ten finishes in the 292 tournaments he had entered. Along the way, Hogan had invented the modern golf swing, but it remained foreign and unattainable by most players at the time.

Under Hogan's guidance, John eagerly embarked on an intense program that completely replaced his former golf swing. He studied and practiced the dynamics of Hogan's "chain action" and the laws of cause and effect that govern the swing. He learned a sequence of specific movements designed to bring the clubhead through the ball with consistent power and accuracy.

Hogan began by fine-tuning John's grip, then showed him a strong setup that John would later adapt and call the "impact address position." John learned how to create a powerful coil by turning his hands, arms, and shoulders around a stationary right knee. They worked on turning John's elbows inward at address and keeping them low and close to the torso throughout the swing. Now, instead of getting handsy, John had to learn to let his hands remain passive and follow his arms as his upper body uncoiled through the ball.

Hogan often reminded John that whether you have a chance to shoot your career best or win the U.S. Open, you must possess a sound swing that will continue to perform under pressure. "That's the swing we're working on here," Hogan said.

Along with their workouts on the practice tee and out on the course, Hogan and John spent many hours talking in the grill-room at Shady Oaks. During one of those early sessions, Hogan asked John about his golfing goals. "I want to win five U.S. Opens and finish in the top ten money winners of all time," John replied.

"That's very admirable, John," Hogan said, "but let's see if we can get you ready to make the cut at the L.A. Open next week." (Still in transition from his old swing, John faltered and missed the cut.)

Hogan also instructed John on developing a strong imagination to help manage his game. The game of golf is *played* with one main thought, Hogan said. Visualize the shot you want and "see" it flying toward your target. Once you have practiced and prepared yourself, he continued, go out and enjoy dreaming the ball around the golf course.

John and Hogan usually played only a few holes during each session but always with a specific purpose, whether it was mental for scoring or physical for swing development. During classes at his Maximum Golf Schools, John related the following incident many times.

On one occasion, Hogan was getting ready to hit his ball, and he called John over from the golf cart.

"See this shot I have? This is the most important shot of my life," Hogan told him, pausing momentarily to flick his cigarette to the ground. "This is the only one I have any control over right now. All the swings of the past are just that, the past. All the shots I'll be hitting in the future are irrelevant right now. So, because golf is played in the present, this one shot, right now, is the most important one to me. I will use everything in my power to execute this shot to the best of my ability."

John said it was an amazing moment. The flag was about 145 yards away, and Hogan had an 8-iron in his hands. He set up and hit the shot pure. They tracked the ball's flight and watched as it lipped out and stopped inches from the cup. Hogan smiled and gave John a knowing wink as he strolled back to the cart.

During the early seventies, Hogan continued to share a treasure of insights and techniques with John while they played and talked golf. These tips were given with the understanding that everything that passed between them would be kept in strict confidence. Even during Hogan's retirement from tournament golf, he was still digging in the dirt, and he had no intention of casting his hard-earned pearls into the public arena except on his own terms and with just compensation. These sessions with John were private business, privy to the very few whom Hogan accepted into his inner circle.

Hogan advised John to use this knowledge as raw material to develop and refine his own golf game. John was free to talk about some of their experiences, but during Hogan's lifetime John must never publicly divulge the secrets he was being taught.

When John started his Maximum Golf Schools in 1979, he followed these instructions and adapted Hogan's key ideas into his own teaching program, giving full credit to his teacher. In 1986, he produced a book and a video titled *Maximum Golf*, the only published instructional system based solely on personal experience with Hogan. True to John's commitment, his book withheld confidential information, including the insights Hogan had dug up *after* his own book, *Five Lessons: The Modern Fundamentals of Golf*, came out in 1957.

John gave me the task of making sure that the revelations he had kept under cover would be chronicled for posterity, along with some of his other experiences with Hogan. I have done that in this book. From the beginning, I have validated these teachings time after time in my own game and with countless students. We are living proof that Hogan's magic can be learned and applied successfully by any dedicated golfer of average talent.

The Master's Tricks of the Trade

As John continued receiving his instruction at the feet of the master, he also learned certain subtle aspects of Hogan's techniques, along with intriguing new ways to see and play the game. John often called them Hogan's "tricks of the trade." These fascinating gems reveal the range of Hogan's imagination and his determination to perfect his game, which continued until his final breath.

Don't Look Back

On one occasion after Hogan hit a less-than-perfect shot, he momentarily furrowed his brow in a sign of displeasure. When he regained composure, he told John of an important technique he'd developed to deal with disappointment. Hogan described how he walked the golf course imagining an enormous impenetrable wall following right behind him. This wall extended to either side as far as the eye could see and from the earth up into the heavens. The wall moved with his every step and blocked his view of everything that had occurred before the present moment.

Once the shot is played, it becomes history, never to be changed, Ben told John. So why look back? The lesson should already be absorbed and be a part of you. History is useful only until you grasp what it has to teach you. Let the teacher, the experience, fade away after it accomplishes its purpose.

When you make a mistake, Hogan said, quickly accept it as your instruction and then move on. Concentrate all of your attention on the next opportunity to make a terrific shot.

Looking Back at the Future

"If you want to see the proper landing areas for the par fours and the par fives, Ben said you must walk the course backward," John recalled. "That way, you can find the best position to approach the green, depending on where the pin is located. Once you discover those spots, you can step off the distance to the tee and determine if you need to use your driver or another club to hit to the optimum area."

John added, "Many courses can have a hilly terrain, and Ben felt that the golf course designer almost always establishes flat spots intended for positioning yourself off the tee. He said the only sure way to see these flat spots is to view them from out on the fairway looking back toward the tee."

One day John and Hogan were playing at Shady Oaks, and they came to the tee of a par five. Ben gestured to John to stay in the cart because they were going for a little ride. They drove to the top of a rise in the fairway about 265 yards from the tee and got out of the cart. Ben took out his 5-iron and surveyed the area for a moment. Then he walked over to a flat spot and axed the club-head into the turf. He said that was the target spot the architect had designed to give golfers the best chance to get home in two.

With his point made, Hogan said they should now go back and play the hole. They were returning to the cart when Hogan stopped, turned, and walked back to the flat spot. He took a tee from his front pocket, bent down, and fixed the gouge he'd just made. "I was thinking how thoughtful he was to repair his mark," John said, "but as Ben stood up, he told me he didn't want a bad lie for his second shot."

This common ritual was typical of Hogan's thoroughness in preparing for tournaments. During his practice rounds for the British Open at Carnoustie in 1953, he walked that course backward—from the 18th green to the first tee—many evenings after dinner. He was memorizing hazard locations, fairway and green undulations, and optimum landing areas for his tee shots. Records show that in 108 holes of play at Carnoustie, his ball landed in the rough only once during a practice round.

Worst Ball

Hogan told John of a challenging but enjoyable game he called "worst ball." He said it's guaranteed to turn any golf course you've played into an entirely new adventure. This exercise is exactly the reverse of a scramble format, where you take the best shot of the twosome or foursome and each play from there.

Worst ball is played not as a team but individually. Each player starts by hitting two shots from the tee and picking the worst outcome. Then you hit two balls from that point, pick the worst shot and hit two more, and so on until you reach the green.

Once on the putting surface, you must make two putts from the same spot to finish the hole. No matter how great a putt you pull off, you must execute it twice in a row for the shot to count.

Hogan recommended this playing drill to John as a way to

gauge his scoring skills. He said it would help hone John's ability to concentrate and would keep the pressure on to execute consistently well. "If you can score even par playing worst ball," Hogan said, "you're ready for tournament golf."

Different Shots, Same Swing

During one of their earlier sessions, John asked Hogan about working the ball left and right. Hogan told him to hit four different shots: high draw, low draw, high fade, and low fade. John performed them adequately. Then Hogan pointed out that John had used four different swings and that under any pressure, they would fold like a deck of cards.

Hogan gave John one of his famous laser-eye looks and said, "Life is too short to perfect one swing, let alone different swings to draw or fade the ball. We are creating a machine, your machine, where your hands are the chuck and the club is the tool. If you want to work the ball, turn the tool in the chuck. Never alter the mechanics of your machine to alter the direction of the shot."

Think about it a moment, and you'll see how simple it is, he told John. You draw or fade the ball simply by adjusting your stance while keeping the clubface square to the target line. (Tiger Woods presented this same basic method in one of his *Golf Digest* instructional features. Unlike Hogan, however, Tiger appears to have mastered several variations of his golf swing, and he usually performs them quite well in competition.)

Hogan then explained how to get a variety of shots with the same basic swing.

- **Fade:** Align your stance—feet, shoulders, arms—slightly to the left of the target line. Turn the club ("tool") in your hands ("chuck") so that the clubface is aimed straight toward the target. Use your regular swing. The club should follow the line of your stance and cut across the ball, putting a clockwise sidespin on it, thus causing it to fade to the right. The ball should start out heading left of the target line, then curve back toward the center.

- **Draw:** Do the reverse of the fade. Align your stance slightly to the right, but set the clubface square to the target line. Use your regular swing. The clubface should follow the line of your stance and put a counterclockwise overspin on the ball, thus causing a draw to the left. The ball should start off to the right and curve back toward the center.

- **Low shots:** Position the ball back in the stance so that the clubface meets the ball as it descends to the bottom of the swing arc, thus keeping the ball down on a lower flight path.

- **High shots:** Position the ball slightly forward in the stance so that the clubface meets the ball at the bottom of the arc, thus lifting the ball into a higher flight path. (In a normal swing, the bottom of the arc usually is reached *after* the club strikes the ball and continues downward to take a divot.)

Hogan told John that he could fine-tune the ball's behavior by practicing to see how much to realign the stance and ball position to get the precise shot he wanted. He reminded John that while the setup may be adjusted, the same swing movements should be used for every shot.

Understanding Centrifugal Force

One day John led me into the backyard of his home in the suburbs of southern California. He lived in a residential community of Carlsbad, where the houses are high on a hill and everyone on his side of the street had an open view of the surrounding mountains and hillsides.

Evidence of John's handiwork graced the entire backyard. He was the kind of guy who had to stay busy, and if he wasn't teaching golf, he was building something. He designed and constructed an impressive gazebo in the back right corner, where he and his wife, Gay, had exchanged their wedding vows. He also built a cascading waterfall and a flowing stream, complete with a small walking bridge, that dissected the neatly manicured lawn.

We met this way quite often, especially during my first year of intensive training in the Maximum Golf School teaching system. Since John didn't engage in follow-up sessions with his students after each school, he increasingly relied on me to handle that responsibility. He wanted to be certain that I received a thorough understanding of all the principles and techniques in his curriculum.

John ushered me over to the patio, where he explained my lesson for the day. He said that Hogan often pulled him aside to point out a particular movement in the swing. Today, for me, it was the right elbow.

John kept a bushel of odd clubs nearby for practicing his swing or launching old golf balls out into the hills. Across the yard, a fence stood guard over a cliff that dropped down about sixty feet into an area occupied by an elementary school. John told me that he often hit balls from the ledge of the cliff, but only well after school hours, in case he hit a fat shot or two.

He grabbed one of the clubs and said, "Watch this. Hogan showed me this exercise to illustrate the importance of the right elbow in the swing."

John took his regular grip and addressed an imaginary ball.

Then he removed his left hand from the club. He swung the club back to about a three-quarter turn, initiated his downswing, and as he turned through the impact zone, he released the club into the blue yonder.

(Hogan credited this exercise to Jack Burke Sr., whose golf students included Babe Zaharias, Henry Picard, Jimmy Demaret, Jack Grout, and Jack Burke Jr. In the exercise, Jack Burke Sr. had his students take the club back, start the downswing, and then, as it came through the hitting area, release their grip and let the club fly out onto the practice range. Jack Jr. would run out and shag the clubs. The throwing sensation enabled his pupils to feel a smooth swing tempo and the flowing power of a full release *through* the ball to the finish. Hogan revised this exercise by taking the left hand off the club so that he could highlight the function of the right elbow. Decades later, in his book *Extraordinary Golf*, Fred Shoemaker featured this same club-throwing technique that Burke had originated in the 1940s.)

"See that?" John asked, as we both watched the club bounce off the fence. "If you load the right elbow on the way down and let the lower body lead into the hitting area properly, centrifugal force releases the club as you continue turning around your spine toward your target."

"Loading the right elbow" is how Hogan described the function of the right arm in the downswing. When you "load," you drop the right elbow into the right hip, where it compresses as the body turns. The right elbow becomes a pivot around which the arms and hands unleash the clubhead through the ball. This happens naturally if the arms and hands remain passive and follow the body's turn.

Looks easy enough, I thought. So I grabbed one of the old clubs and readied myself to give it a heave. I loaded pretty well and kept my right elbow close in to my torso as I turned back and then started my downswing. When I came into the hitting area, though, my elbow came up and out, my right hand collapsed, and the golf club flew off to the left, where it bashed into a large, dense bush.

"What happened?" I asked.

"Same thing that happened to me the first time I tried," John reassured me. "You have to continue leading with the right elbow all the way *through* the hitting area, not just *to* it. When your turn reaches the center point of the swing, centrifugal force takes over and releases the club straight toward the target.

"Later, when you grip properly with both hands, this movement automatically uncocks your right hand as it flings the clubhead through the ball. This exercise is to help you get the feeling of how the right elbow stays in tight through the downswing and how the hands get released automatically through the hitting area."

I tried it again, and the club dove straight into the same bush.

John smiled and said, "That's okay. You'll get the hang of it soon enough."

I tried for the rest of the afternoon, throwing those stupid clubs and then going to pick them up. I was amazed at what a struggle it was to get the right elbow to stay close in to my torso and let the release happen by itself. After I don't know how many throws, I finally relaxed enough to rely on the power of my body's turn to do the trick. The feeling of fluidity in the movement was something I'd never before experienced. Best of all, I felt that rare sense of breaking new ground and entering a new dimension of knowledge hidden from me before that moment.

I immediately began to incorporate the flowing impression I received from throwing clubs into the act of swinging *through* the golf ball. In the past, most of my energy had been directed at the ball, and I felt that the direction of its flight was controlled only by where I aimed. Now, however, with this new understanding of how to employ the right elbow, my body felt like a coordinated machine that would propel my turn through the ball with explosive energy straight toward the target. My right arm wasn't wandering out and "over the top" anymore. I was thrilled to experience this phase of Hogan's famous "chain action" and feel how it kept my swing on line with new power and consistency.

That, in itself, was a huge improvement. When John later taught me how to incorporate the proper use of the left arm into this movement (see the next section), the sensation of being connected and in control as I unwind in the hitting area was, and continues to be, phenomenal.

Getting a Grip on the Missing Link

Shortly after John narrowly missed hitting into an array of plate-glass windows during an earlier session with Hogan, he began to feel devastated at the thought of changing his grip to Hogan's recommended weak hand position. He despaired that he'd hit everything right with no end in sight. So he went back to Hogan the next day for a "grillroom chat," in hopes of finding a solution.

Hogan was at his customary corner table having a bite to eat, and he invited John to join him. John sat down and described his dilemma. Hogan thought a moment and told John that he must *want* to change his grip or the change would never fully take place. The old grip would tend to come back little by little, and, eventually, John would end up with the same strong hand position he'd had when they first met.

"I fought it for years," Hogan said.

John still didn't feel comfortable with the idea and asked how he could make himself *want* to change to a grip that felt weak and out of control.

"I'll show you after we eat our lunch," Ben said. They finished eating and went out to the practice tee, where Ben told John to get his 7-iron and to set up in his normal stance, with flexed legs and a straight spine angle. Hogan turned John's elbows inward until they pointed toward the hips but told him to take his regular strong grip. Hogan asked him how he felt. John said he was fine.

Then Hogan said, "Take the club back halfway until your hands reach hip level and then stop." John obliged.

Hogan came over and told him to start the downswing with the lower body and he would guide John's hands and arms into the hitting area. When John's hands approached the impact zone, Hogan took John's left elbow and started turning it toward his left hip. John said he felt the back of his left hand and the palm of his right hand turn toward the ground.

"See that?" Hogan said. "When the left elbow turns inward and gets out of the way, the hands can work properly without interference. The only problem is the position of the clubface. Where is it pointed?"

John saw that it was pointed left of his target.

Hogan explained that if you swing properly with a strong grip, the clubface will be closed every time as it enters the impact zone. At this point, he continued, there are only two ways to keep the clubface square to your line: (1) change your grip and let the left elbow do its job, or (2) return to the old sliding motion, a move that robs you of power and requires you to get "handsy" again to control the clubface.

"I suggest you do what I did and start by modifying your

grip," Hogan said. "The grip is the foundation that sets up the rest of your swing. It's the only dependable way to control your club in pressure situations."

John said he started hitting short shots using the new weak grip, making sure the left elbow turned in to square the club-face. Then he moved on to full shots. In the beginning, he hooked a lot of balls because he unconsciously kept reverting to his old stronger grip, but his determination and practice began to keep his hands in line and make this left elbow move feel natural and reliable. Soon it became something he could count on, a certain way to keep the clubface on line with the target, time after time.

Now that he understood the wisdom of the weaker hand position on the club and how the clubface is controlled by the left elbow, John said he *wanted* to change his grip.

John told me that very few people understand the importance of this simple but essential movement. Recently, after a lifetime of observing endless analyses of Hogan's swing by teaching gurus and players alike, I realized that the role of the left elbow is the missing link in the search for Hogan's complete "secret." It's the final step that, to my knowledge, only a handful—Ken Venturi, for one—have ever understood and no one has ever brought forth in a complete analysis of Hogan's swing.

Some contemporary analysts and instructors have observed that Hogan didn't keep his own elbows turned inward at address or throughout the swing. This is true for the post-accident Hogan swing and for part of his earlier days, when he was just discovering the importance of this move. Hogan's body was badly beaten in the head-on bus collision in 1949, especially his shoulders, collarbone, pelvis, knees, and left ankle. He told John that he could no longer set up or swing the way he wanted to because of the pain and the way his bones had healed. He said that he had to train himself to bring his elbows closer together after his swing was underway because he couldn't do it during the setup.

In a masterful remake, Hogan had modified elements of his swing to accommodate his crippled body. Yet he emphatically warned John not to mimic his current swing but to learn the fundamental movements Hogan was now teaching him. "I'm showing you the swing I would be using now if I were physically capable," he told John.

One of my great joys in teaching is when golfers come to me with their slicing woes. I've helped hundreds of players cure this persistent nemesis. I've had them hitting a nice little draw within minutes after I showed them how to turn the left elbow inward and let the hands follow the arms into the impact zone. It's one of those "Bingo!" moments where once you see it happen, you realize that this profound little move has been here all along, just waiting to be discovered and put to work.

It's been said that a true genius makes complex things simple, and that's what Hogan did with this left elbow move.

Pronation and Supination

One day John asked Ben, "I have to admit, I really don't understand much about pronation and supination. What are they, and what do you do with them?"

"Forget about all that," Hogan said bluntly. "They're just words for what happens when you swing correctly. When you set your arms and elbows inward and let your shoulders move them as your body turns, the hands will tend to pronate and supinate naturally."

Pronate means "to turn or face downward." *Supinate* means "to turn or face upward." Technically, during the backswing, the left hand pronates and the right hand supinates. The opposite occurs on the downswing. These are correct definitions but are usually too complicated to visualize—no wonder Hogan advised John to "forget about all that."

Hogan emphasized that the movement, not what you call it, is what's important. He then described the actions to take for correct hand movement.

On the backswing, roll the hands clockwise and keep the elbows close together and tight to the torso as you turn properly around your spine. Hogan told John to observe how he immediately rolls his hands to the right to initiate his swing. He said this hand action sets up a powerful return move and increases clubhead speed by a significant amount. He also gives his left wrist a slight twist inward as further insurance that he won't hook the ball.

On the downswing, Hogan added, simply let the hands be relaxed and passive. Correct rotation of the arms and elbows will return the hands to their original setup position and will bring the clubface straight through the ball.

Hogan was adamant that the only tasks for the hands are to grip the club properly, cock the wrists, and *follow* the arms—not to direct the club through the swing. That way, the hands assume their proper role in the chain action that Hogan describes in his *Five Lessons: The Modern Fundamentals of Golf.*

Call it what you may, Hogan said, this series of movements is the only certain way to consistently square up the clubface under the pressure of tournament play. (More on this in chapter 6, "The Legendary Golf System.")

o o o

The key to understanding the many facets of Hogan's secret, John emphasized, is that all components in the chain action must be used in concert as an integrated system for the swing to work effectively. And when they are used together, he said, it's almost like being in Hogan's shoes and experiencing the unimaginable thrill of his powerful, flawless golf swing.

2

Maximum Golf:
The Front Nine

The Teacher and the Students

John Schlee could not imagine a life without golf when his back condition forced him to retire as a playing professional in 1978. Dropping out of the PGA Tour meant a rapid descent to earth from the pinnacle of world-class golf. No more applause and adulation, no more perks and pampering, no more opportunities to play for fame and fortune. Somehow, he had to find a new way to reroute himself within the only game that gave him satisfaction and an outlet for his passion.

The most logical and appealing option was to teach others what he had learned as one of Hogan's few disciples and from twelve years competing on the Tour. He'd finished forty-sixth on the all-time money list, and, while not a household name, he enjoyed modest notoriety as a colorful character on and off the course. John felt confident in his appeal as a golf teacher who had "been there" and could show his students the real thing.

So in 1979, brimming with his characteristic enthusiasm for new adventures, John began laying plans to start a golf school. His first move was to immortalize his credentials. He went directly to Hogan and asked for the master's endorsement, along with the use of his name.

In typical fashion, Hogan was quiet for a long moment and then said, "John, my name is all I have. I've worked all my life to develop adjectives that would please me when my name is mentioned. . . . I think it's time for you to start building your own adjectives. And so, my answer is no. Go build your name, and love doing it."

Hogan gave John another piece of advice: "Have your school in one location. Don't become a traveling circus, because you're not going to attract the people who really want to learn. Make people come to you."

A bit disappointed but undeterred, John drove straight ahead and started putting the details together. He named his enterprise the Maximum Golf School. It would become a perfect reflection of his personal style: total commitment and focus, an aggressive schedule of hard work, and innovative instructional methods, with primary emphasis on the fundamentals of the Hogan golf swing and how to perform them consistently.

In 1979, John set up shop in Hawaii, where he had won his only Tour victory. Within a year, he moved to Industry Hills, California, to tap into the larger stateside student market. John recruited an excellent assistant in Gregg Graham, a pro at Industry Hills G.C. who worked and studied under another renowned player and teacher, Johnny Revolta.

Still not satisfied with the location, John kept looking until 1984, when he found the school's permanent home at the

Olympic Resort Hotel practice facility in Carlsbad, California, the new haven for golf equipment companies.

It was here that John blossomed into the teacher whom professionals and amateurs would seek out for insights handed down from the "Legend." His Tour record was respectable, with one victory and his near brush with fame at Johnny Miller's 1973 U.S. Open, but the big draw was based on players' awareness that John held some secret knowledge he'd gathered during his years of personal instruction from Ben Hogan. Phil Mickelson, Tom Lehman, David Ogrin, and Gary Hallberg are among those I am aware of who came by to see John. I'm sure many others had picked John's mind before I arrived on the scene a few years after he started the Maximum Golf School.

Maximum Golf sessions were not leisurely social gatherings or executive retreats designed to help harried people unwind. We put our students through a rigorous training regimen that left them creaking and groaning but well introduced to the concepts and mechanics of our system.

Sometimes our intensity surprised a few students, who dropped out to seek a more casual approach for their golf lessons. We knew that those who stayed to finish were serious about their game.

We conducted classes at the Olympic Resort Hotel facility throughout the year, twice a month every other weekend, Friday through Sunday. John insisted on the stretch between schools so he could recuperate. He put a lot of effort into each class and was always "on" throughout the weekend. Daily sessions started promptly at 9 A.M. and finished at 5 P.M., with classroom time each morning and range work in the afternoons.

We attracted students from across the nation through large ads in *Golf Digest* and *GOLF* magazine. After John and Acorn Sports got together to produce the Maximum Golf Teaching System (book, video, and audiotapes), most of our students came from sales of the system.

John set a limit of twenty participants per school and employed three assistant instructors: Bruce Petz, Lin Wicks, and me. Gregg Graham, who moved from Industry Hills to Hacienda Heights in La Habra Heights, California, joined us if we had the maximum number of students.

Getting Motivated

My first three-day school, compliments of John, left me feeling overwhelmed. I'd just experienced my first glimpse of an entirely new dimension of golf knowledge. It was far more than I had imagined, and my mind was spinning. I was a pretty fair golfer, but this session opened doors I didn't even know existed about the golf swing in general and Ben Hogan in particular. I felt like a dry sponge and couldn't wait to soak up every iota of knowledge pouring out of the classroom and saturating the atmosphere of John's school.

The game of golf never came naturally to me. I constantly searched for ways to perform good swing movements, studying other players on the course, on television, and in all the videos and books stacked on my tabletops and shelves. I usually encountered a problem that's common to most golfers: I could see *what* to do, but rarely did players or instructors give me a good understanding of *how* or *why* to do it.

John was answering these questions for me. I remember the

excitement of thinking, Finally, I've found the real thing here, and it's the only place I want to be right now.

After the session ended, John encouraged me to hang around with him the rest of the week, whenever I was free, to ask him questions and begin to assimilate the swing principles and insights he'd accumulated from Hogan and his own days on the Tour. I felt as if fate had already decided for us, and, without any formal declarations, there was no question that I would stay on as his assistant. I was still working nights in a local restaurant but had no trouble rolling out of bed early every day for this, my real job.

About a week into my apprenticeship, I asked John for help in understanding how to move my body through the hitting area. I had been caught up in the popular slide-and-hit-the-wall motion, and I wasn't quite comfortable swinging with a full turn around my spine, as John had shown us in classes. He studied me briefly and said, "I have just what you're looking for." He went over to the main desk in the office and pulled a pamphlet titled *Maximum Golf Motivators* from the top drawer.

"Here," John said, as he introduced me to my new assistants. "They're in the garage. Grab what you want and wear them out." I scanned the pamphlet and then went out to the garage, where I found a mixed collection of self-help contraptions. I picked out three of them: the arm stabilizer, the right knee holder, and the Secret. When I checked them out with John, he told me to become familiar with these gizmos because they all related to key elements of Ben Hogan's swing.

The arm stabilizer held your arms close to the body and close together. It was tight and awkward at first, but with regular practice my arms soon felt natural and comfortable in this position. Hogan had stressed time and again how crucial it is to keep the arms close together, with the elbows turned inward and tight to the torso. His reminder that "the arms should work as one big arm" gave me a good visual idea of what this stabilizer was supposed to teach me. Once I got it, I felt a previously unknown confidence in the new power and reliability of my swing. (We'll go over this movement and other essentials in chapter 5.)

The right knee holder was designed to keep the right knee turned slightly inward and flexed throughout the backswing. This was a key part of John's renowned "impact position" setup that he had adapted from Hogan's instruction. It also kept the weight shift pushing into the inside of my rear foot, making it almost impossible to slide into the backswing or roll over to the outside of my foot. This gadget helped me to develop a strong coil and maintain a firm, balanced foundation throughout the swing.

My favorite gizmo was called the Secret. Made of molded plastic, it wrapped around the right wrist and was secured with Velcro straps. It held the right wrist in a cupped position (bent, angled back). This gadget helped prevent a premature release of the hands by making them *follow* the arms into the hitting area, another essential key in Hogan's swing technique.

John created this product for two fundamental reasons. First, it keeps the hands from leading the downswing, which helps to eliminate the "over the top" or casting motion. Second, it adds power by keeping the right wrist cocked to promote a strong move into the back of the ball—as if you were hitting it with the palm of your right hand—as the club whips through the impact area.

Gregg Graham described how John invented the Secret one day during a classroom session: "John was trying to show some students how Hogan's emphasis on retaining the right wrist angle added power to the golf swing. John suddenly got up from his chair and started searching for something to hold his right wrist in Hogan's cupped position. He found a couple of wooden tongue depressors from a first-aid kit and borrowed some Scotch tape from a waitress. John then fashioned a crude model of the Secret and attached it to his own right hand. 'This,' he told the amused group, 'is what we're looking for.'"

John was convinced that such a teaching device would help the average golfer understand a crucial role of the right hand and the wrist in the golf swing. One of his students that day pledged the monetary backing to produce his Secret, and suddenly John was in business.

John's spontaneity was so typical of his modus operandi: jump all over a good idea, find ways to make it work, and run as far as he could with it. He saw his world as an endless field of opportunities to be resourceful and to create what he wanted. I never heard him use the word *problem* or *solution*.

The three Motivators were sold through Maximum Golf School advertising in *Golf Digest* and *GOLF* magazine, mainly during the early 1980s. When the school site moved from Industry Hills to Carlsbad, John had a small supply of these gadgets and sold them to interested students as souvenir learning aids. He never developed a nationwide sales plan, though, and none of these Motivators ever made it to the mass market. The few remaining ones ended up in John's garage.

Greg Norman later obtained rights to the Secret from John's family and released his version in the mid-1990s.

These learning tools—the arm stabilizer, the right knee holder, and the Secret—helped me to develop Hogan's fundamental swing motions, which I've practiced for years and still teach in my training seminars today. I was never that interested in golf gimmicks that you try to plug into your generic golf swing, but these Motivators really did the job. Best of all, they worked together as part of an integrated learning system based on a real master's golf swing.

Maximum School Days

In the spring of 1985, John was in the middle of finishing his *Maximum Golf* instructional book when I arrived on the scene. I was always first in line to talk with him about his book and teaching philosophy. John quickly became aware of my intense interest and he appreciated having someone on hand who really cared about what he had to offer. Before shipping chapters off to his publisher, John often asked me to edit them, and, to my surprise, he seemed to respect my suggestions.

Writing was not a labor John loved, mainly because of his dyslexia. For his entire life, it had been a struggle for him to read and write. The blessing within this handicap is that he naturally found it easier to transform ideas directly into action, from head to hands, with only enough words to communicate the bare essentials. You never got a letter or a memo from John, but he did have huge telephone bills. I didn't realize until later what a phenomenal achievement it had been for him to transfer his teachings into book form.

When it came time to shoot the video portion of the Maximum Golf System, he asked me to be the technical director on the set. I concentrated on the video monitor and listened to the audio to make sure we followed our plan during filming. When the video filming was completed, I joined John in the editing booth for five days to coordinate the final two-hour production.

When classes were in session, John made it quite clear who

was in charge, and he had little patience for chitchat or other distractions. More than once, John got out his checkbook, returned a student's enrollment fee, and sent him packing. He was an intense, focused teacher who truly cared about his students. I often saw him make the extra effort to help anyone who was sincerely trying to understand.

Yet he could be merciless with people who violated the code of paying perfect, willing attention to his instruction. In one incident, John was laying the foundation of a point Hogan had made about the lower body when a student named Bill (who was prematurely bald) rudely and loudly voiced his objections about John's interpretation of Hogan's methods. It went like this:

One Friday morning, John began instructing in the usual manner by explaining Hogan's ideas on leg and hip action during the setup and the swing. "When you set up correctly in the 'impact address position,' slightly more weight will be on the left foot than on the right foot," John said.

"Hogan didn't have more weight on his left side at address," Bill interjected loudly from the back of the room.

John ignored this outburst and continued. "This weight distribution helps you come into the impact zone with more weight on the left side than the right, exactly where it should be."

Bill countered with another outburst. "Why didn't Hogan mention this in his *Five Lessons* book?" Ordinarily, that might be a point worth discussing, but Bill's tone was clearly contentious.

I could see from the expression in John's eyes that he'd had enough of this guy. John went right into attack mode by calling him out and asking him a completely unrelated question: "Bill, I always wondered something about men who are bald. When you wash your face, where do you stop?" John made a washing motion with his hands in front of his face and continued up past his forehead. He took on a mock bewildered look as he stared straight at Bill. This produced a few snickers but otherwise sent a message that John ran the classroom, and if you didn't respect that, he could lash out and embarrass you in front of the other classmates. Where someone else might have marched out of class in a huff, a stunned Bill wilted in his seat and said no more.

Just before the outdoor session began, John pulled Bill aside to patch things up and explain in more detail Hogan's ideas on the lower body. To Bill's credit and to my amazement, he stayed on and became a model student for the rest of the weekend.

○ ○ ○

Hogan had stressed to John that for something to be accepted as true, it had to be based on sound reasoning. In golf, he said, you must understand the *why's* of the swing. Being told to do something because "all good players do it" is not a valid reason. Answering the what, why, and how of every move in the golf swing was a cornerstone of John's teaching style that distinguished him from so many other instructors.

For example, one key factor in Hogan's teachings is the importance of the arms and elbows being set as close together as possible at address and during the swing. In the classroom setting, John emphasized the arms as the *what*. John explained *why* we keep the arms close, saying, "Setting the elbows inward allows the arms to work together as a single unit. This is especially important on the downswing, when the spinning torso releases its energy outward through the arms as the proper elbow movement automatically brings the clubhead square to the target."

John also pointed out some of the detriments of *not* following Hogan's advice, such as, "Allowing the arms to work independently of one another will result in pushes to the right if the left arm wins the battle for dominance or pulls to the left if the right arm wins [for right-handers]."

In learning the *how* of the inward set of the arms, John said that Hogan suggested using a tennis ball. Place the ball nearby on a countertop or a table. With your hands in a proper grip on the golf club, pick up the ball by squeezing it between your forearms. You should be able to swing the club back at least to hip level and swing back through the hitting area to about hip level without dropping the ball.

John often told his students, "I don't care what you are learning; if the teacher doesn't give you a good enough reason to do something, go learn somewhere else. But when you do try something, always give it your best."

Always doing your best seemed like an old cliché to me until John explained an enlightening encounter he'd had with one of his high school coaches. The coach had asked him, "So John, how are you doing in your schoolwork?"

"I'm doing enough to get by," John replied "I'm middle of the road, a couple of Bs, a few Cs, a couple Ds."

The coach persisted with John, "Is that okay with you? I mean, you're always excelling in sports. You're a great runner, a great hitter, and a super golfer. You like being right there in the middle with your studies?"

John shrugged. "Yeah, sure, it's average."

The coach then said, "Let me give you a definition of average: *Average is the best of the worst or worst of the best.* Now which category do you want to be in?"

John told me that the coach's definition woke him up and changed his whole outlook on life. The new attitude didn't affect his grades that much, but it made him think twice about other activities in his life. He said he finally realized that no matter what you are doing—hitting a golf shot, planting a rosebush, or washing your car—always do it to the best of your ability, because *success in one area of your life breeds success in other areas.* John had never understood that connection before, and neither had I.

○ ○ ○

During the next few years, we continued to look for better ways to school our students on the Hogan philosophy and swing concepts. John designed and constructed a private practice tee at Olympic's practice range, complete with redwood benches and deck with video camera mounts and a redwood canopy for shade. It was located at the far end of the existing range and gave our students a secluded place to work.

John soon noticed my ability to analyze a student's swing on the video monitor, and he gave me the title of First Assistant, with responsibility for all final swing evaluations.

Eventually, I worked my way into the Maximum Golf School office, and I could finally quit my night job at the restaurant. Along with my teaching duties, I began helping John's wife, Gay, with booking new and follow-up students, as well as answering telephone inquiries about the school and questions about our teaching methods.

John also passed all the individual lessons my way, which I appreciated as an act of confidence in my abilities, but I knew that, like Hogan, John didn't have the patience or the inclination to deal with students on a one-on-one basis.

I started a weekend follow-up school to help students practice our classroom material on the golf course. The playing school was limited to three former students who had completed our regular three-day course. We worked on the practice tee in the morning and played nine holes together in the afternoon, with emphasis on course management insights that Hogan had taught John. This was a popular follow-up with students and a worthwhile addition to our curriculum.

During my tenure, I estimate that about 2,200 students of all shapes and dispositions came through our doors. One of my favorites was a gentleman named Milt who was ninety-three years old and came looking for "a few extra yards." Milt and I hit it off right away, and we enjoyed some interesting chats throughout the weekend.

One day I asked Milt about the 1910 Halley's comet (this was around the time of its 1986 appearance). "Oh, yes," he said. "I was about seventeen, and I remember how that comet really lit up the sky. People had all kinds of opinions about it." Any time I got the chance, I hung out with Milt, helping him gain those few extra yards and picking his brain about the Wright brothers and Henry Ford.

Most of the other students were businessmen, fathers, and golf junkies. We did have a number of women come through the school, but the male-female ratio was about 6 to 1.

Keeping Score

I always felt privileged when I could get out and play golf with John on a few courses in the San Diego area. It gave me a chance to see the teacher demonstrate the lessons we covered in school and to have some fun times with the boss.

With his main emphasis on running the school, John's own game had gotten a little rusty since he'd left the Tour. When we first started playing together, I was surprised that my drives regularly blew 20 yards past his. I was hitting them around 265 yards on average. As John got more serious about tuning up for his Senior Tour debut, though, his coordination came back, along with his length and accuracy. My days of "bragging rights" were over as he started pounding the ball 275 to 300 yards. His driving was impressive even by today's standards.

John loved to hit driver, especially off the fairway. He could pinch the ball and make it rocket out on a low trajectory, then rise like an airplane taking off. That was partly the balata ball but mostly the way he captured it perfectly at the bottom of the arc. Before he'd met Hogan, John's lack of directional control left him all over the place, even with the short clubs. Now he could fire his 3-iron shots straight out there around 220 yards.

John had a master's touch around the greens and rarely failed to get up and down inside 50 yards. His putting, which used to make Hogan burn with envy, was always phenomenal. He dropped 25-footers like today's top players make 8-footers. John, a meticulous record keeper, said he documented only one three-putt during his 1973–1974 seasons on Tour. Hogan used to say that if his head was on Tommy Bolt's body, they'd win everything. I can safely say that if Hogan could have putted like John, he would have won at least four more U.S. Opens, four more Masters, and God knows how many others.

On the playing field I also learned a lot about John's character, which, in addition to his impetuous nature, included a real soft spot for people less fortunate.

John often called a country club and told them who he was, asking if he could bring out a foursome when the course wasn't busy, usually in the afternoons. When we arrived, he immediately went to the pro shop to thank them for letting us play. He always got our greens fees comped. Then he quickly browsed through the shop, picked out some golf balls and visors for us, and paid the pro or the assistant in cash.

The first time it happened, John told us, "I'm sure you don't need another visor; you probably have as many as I do. But if they comp us to play their golf course and use their golf carts, I like to show my appreciation by getting something in their shop. They need to earn a living the same as the next guy, and I like to help these boys out whenever I can." He said that we'd be surprised at how many touring professionals treat the club pros like second-class citizens.

We played quite a few times over the years, and, like John's time with Hogan, most often it would be only a few holes for some instructional purpose. One afternoon we were playing Shadowridge C.C. in North San Diego County, where I was a member. (The head pro, Hank George, and his assistants Jimmy Letourneau and Rusty Van Dam, were always generous in extending John playing privileges. They also allowed us carte blanche use of the course to shoot our Maximum Golf video.) We were banging it around when John had to leave for an appointment.

I was keeping score and noticed that he was five under after thirteen holes. I knew he didn't have any idea how well he was doing so I yelled over to him as he was leaving, "Hey John, you know how you stand?"

He looked over and said, "You know I don't pay attention to that. I just hit the ball until it finds the bottom of the cup." I laughed and told him his score. He shrugged and scooted off in his cart to the clubhouse. If I ever got to five under at any point in a round, it would take a bulldozer to get me off the course.

While John enjoyed occasional outings with students and staff, he got his real kicks playing with celebrities. He was a big Yankees fan and got to be playing pals with Mickey Mantle. In fact, Mickey was one of his early financial backers when John was getting started on the PGA Tour. They usually got a round in whenever they happened to be in the same town.

Mickey was hooked on golf and had a true love-hate relationship with the game. Anyone who knew him knew that he had a temper as legendary as his bat. John was reminiscing one day and told me this story about Mickey's wild ways:

"Mickey and I were getting ready to tee off one afternoon when he proposed that we double our wager for the day. I said sure, why not, because I knew Mickey was so competitive and his temper would eventually do him in. I gave him his usual six strokes a side, which was never enough for him to win, and off we went.

"On the first hole, Mickey popped up his drive that left him a long approach shot to the green. While I was watching from the passenger side of the cart—Mickey always wanted to drive— he set up to the ball, took a couple of waggles, and sliced his shot deep into the woods. Uh oh, I thought, here it comes. His temper was always right near the surface and could erupt any time. I didn't realize it just then, but he'd been having a bad day even before he got to the course.

"The next thing I hear is *wham* as his 3-iron hammers into the backside of the golf cart. I jumped in my seat and let out a hoot. He throws down another ball and dubs it a short ways down the fairway. Mickey stomps back over, kicks the rear fender hard and throws his club in the bag. He gets in the cart and gives me this look like, 'If you say one word, I'll treat you like a Bob Gibson fastball.' I wanted to laugh, but I choked it down to a grin and looked straight ahead.

"Mickey kept hitting bad shots, which he routinely followed by kicking and whacking his clubs into various parts of our trusty cart. By the fourth hole, an all-out demolition was in progress. You could easily track where we'd been by following the pieces of smashed fiberglass strewn behind us.

"By the time we finished the ninth hole, we were sitting on what seemed like only the chassis, the battery, and a couple of axles with wheels.

"Mickey drove us right up to the cart park to swap out our wreck. As we clattered into the driveway, an assistant stood there gaping at us. The guy's jaw had sunk into his turtleneck and he looked beyond bewildered. Mickey, still steaming, got out of the cart and walked right over to him. The poor kid looked like he was about to bolt for cover. Mickey stuck his finger an inch from the kid's nose and said, 'Don't say one word. Just put this on my f——ing bill and get us another cart now.'"

After John finished the story, he paused and a wistful look came over his face. "I sure miss Mickey," he said.

○ ○ ○

In early 1988, when we were at the office discussing the coming year, I suggested to John that we needed to write another book detailing his and Hogan's ideas in a more comprehensive instructional system. We had been covering important insights and techniques that hadn't been recorded in John's *Maximum Golf* or in Hogan's books. I thought we should bring everything up to date. Without hesitation, he looked at me and said, "You do it, Tom. You know I don't get along real good with words."

Something in the way he said it suddenly made me realize the fragile, temporal nature of everything Hogan had passed on to John and that he in turn was passing on to me. It finally hit me that John—because of his dyslexia and his frenetic, impatient nature—would never put in writing *everything* he'd learned from Hogan. He hadn't included, among other things, an essential feature of Hogan's golf swing that he'd shown me privately, a missing link that completes the final summary of Hogan's secret.

It now became crystal clear that I was responsible for preserving something of irreplaceable value that might otherwise, after John, pass away and be lost forever. In the midst of this realization, a startling image flashed through my mind. From a distance, I spotted a sparkling diamond the size and shape of a golf ball trickling down a gentle slope. It was rolling toward the edge of a cliff that overlooked the ocean, picking up speed. I started to run after it, and if I didn't get there in time. . . .

That simply could not happen.

I was humbly aware that dozens of other highly qualified people had written, spoken, and taught their versions of the genius and mystery surrounding Ben Hogan's phenomenal mastery of golf. I'd always been in awe of Herbert Warren Wind and the humorous tales of the one and only Dan Jenkins, both intimates of Hogan and his world. Ken Venturi, one of Hogan's favorite playing partners, understood the master as well or better than any other Tour player. The brilliant biographies penned by James Dodson and Curt Sampson have to be the last word on Hogan's life in general. Not to mention the great classics of golf fiction by authors like Steven Pressfield and Michael Murphy, who extol the mystery and the spirit of the game that quietly fueled Hogan's power center.

Who was I to think I could add anything worthwhile to these esteemed conversations?

Yet I was also becoming aware that John had unearthed something truly unique during his years with Hogan, something that less than a handful of people fully comprehended. It was here pulsing in my hands, in my small world, insisting that it be released into a larger world of thirsty minds like mine.

That day I began writing and organizing my notes with a new sense of urgency. Maybe once in a lifetime, if you're very lucky, opportunities like this will fall out of the sky and into your lap. A loud voice in my mind yelled at me, "Do this now before it all slips away!"

Then something out of the blue happened that would change everything.

The Longputter

One day Orville Moody jammed a 2-iron shaft through the top of a grip on a putter called the Taylor Raylor and gave birth to the longputter craze.

It was early March 1988 when Moody and Harold Henning shocked the golf world with record-breaking performances at the Vintage Invitational Senior Golf Tournament. Moody used his makeshift longputter to win by eleven strokes. He became the first golfer to set 18-hole records on two different courses in the same tournament, while setting a Senior Tour record of 263 for 72 holes. Henning, meanwhile, set a Senior record of 129 for the final 36 holes. He shot a 65 on Saturday and a 64 on Sunday, using the longputter for the last 30 holes.

I didn't realize it at the time, but this was the beginning of the end for me. John now had something new to focus his attention on because at that fortuitous moment, he happened to own all of the remaining Taylor Raylors.

Gregg Graham was on hand to witness John's epiphany. "I was staying at John's house that weekend when the longputter craze hit. I distinctly remember getting up Sunday morning and going out to the patio where he was having his morning coffee and reading the sports section. I pulled up a chair and started reaching for some of the paper as I looked over at John. His eyes were wide open and big as saucers. 'Look at this!' he said, as he snapped a page of the sports section toward me. I saw a big feature picture of Orville Moody's Taylor Raylor made into a longputter. Before I could say anything, John looked over at me and said, 'Tom and I are going to be real busy.'"

○ ○ ○

The Taylor Raylor was a standard-sized putter designed by Dr. J. A. Corvi, better known in the aerospace sector for his work with the Apollo space program. With scientifically balanced outer rails extending back from the face of the putter, it could pass for a two-pronged garden hoe.

The design was too radical for prevailing tastes, and after a brief marketing test run, it was discontinued by its manufacturer, TaylorMade. Those few left in circulation gathered dust in their pro shop display racks. Dr. Corvi was too far ahead of his time— if only he could see the putting contrivances they're making today.

John, however, liked the Raylor's heel-toe balanced weighting. Not long before Moody's makeshift invention, John had told Gary Adams, the CEO of TaylorMade, that he would take the remaining stock of about six hundred Raylors off his hands, if the price was right. They made a deal, and this putter transaction continued a friendly relationship that Gary and John enjoyed for many years.

John had known Gary back in the late seventies, when Gary gave birth to the TaylorMade Golf Club Company in his garage in McHenry, Illinois. Gary developed the first "Pittsburgh Persimmon" metal driver and fairway clubs, and he became known as the father of the metalwood revolution. This exciting new technology caused quite a stir when he introduced it at the 1979 PGA merchandise show.

By the late 1980s, TaylorMade had become the top golf equipment company in the world. Gary went on to create two more influential golf companies—Founders Club and McHenry Metals—before he passed away on January 2, 2000.

We had been using our stock of Taylor Raylor putters as parting gifts for students who completed the three-day school. We stopped that immediately when we heard of Orville Moody's victory in Palm Desert.

Maximum Golf promptly became a putter manufacturing company that Sunday. By Monday morning, nearly every pro shop in the country would be calling TaylorMade, which would then inform them that we had the last remaining Taylor Raylors. We in turn would be converting these Raylors into longputters. We'd also enjoy a sudden jump in status as key players in the golf equipment revolution and make a nice haul to the bank.

John's mind was racing. Even with a stock of Raylors on hand, the engineering and logistics of manufacturing and distributing a new line of equipment were daunting. For John, however, this kind of challenge injected new voltage into his belief that he could and would realize any dream that captured his imagination.

We'd need to find or create long shafts and extra grips, design and balance the club, figure out construction specs, and take care of assembly, marketing, packaging, shipping, billing, accounting, and on and on. How could we secure the upper grip and the shaft? How would we ship it? How much should we charge? I distinctly remember asking John about the price because I would be answering the phone come Monday morning when the pro shops found us.

"What do you want to get for the putter?" I asked him.

John thought a few seconds and said, "I don't know, how about $150?"

I thought he was kidding because the average putter in those days cost around $50. What made him think we could get $150?

Nevertheless, we sold all the putters at that price. We also alienated the golf shop professionals by not giving them a decent wholesale cost so they could make a few bucks. I heard more than my share of foul language over the phone and "Who the hell does this John Schlee think he is?" (I often wondered how John's approach to business had turned his formerly compassionate attitude toward club pros into tough, low-margin deals for them.)

John set the standard for pricing longputters, and, despite howls from retailers, it held. Other club manufacturers joined the bonanza, and the new benchmark settled at $125 to $150. The cost of regular putters soon followed suit.

○ ○ ○

My role in our school over the next few months changed quickly. I was now the order taker, clubmaker, shipper, and follow-up person, in addition to my diminishing duties for the golf school, which was dying by the wayside. John gave me the title of VP of marketing and awarded me shares of stock in the newly formed company, the Maximum Golf Corporation.

Things were happening fast. John designed a new putter line similar to the Taylor Raylors, which were long gone. We labeled them the Maximum Golf Longputter 1.3 models, because they were 1.3 pounds. Yes, a lumbering one point three pounds. The shaft had to be stiffer to support the extra weight, so John went to a ski pole manufacturer and had poles designed to use as shafts for the new putters.

John even developed a two-piece model with a threaded insert above the lower grip so that players could take them apart and pack them in their bags when traveling. The USGA didn't approve, however, and quickly reinforced its stance on the one-piece rule. Consequently, the detachable longputters were deemed illegal for USGA play.

By the end of 1988, we had produced our first instructional video to demonstrate how to use the longputter, and we included a copy with each sale. We also secured a spot in Austad's catalog. Austad's Golf, Inc., was one of golf's premiere merchandising companies at the time.

Along the way, we attracted some pretty famous admirers. One day while I was in charge of the office phones, a gentleman who had purchased one of our longputters called. He was an older man from Texas and needed some help with the claw grip. I explained that by placing the grip in the gap between the index finger and the middle finger of the right hand and against the palm, you can guide the putter through the stroke without manipulating the clubface, thereby keeping the face square as it passes through the ball.

He then asked, "Who am I speaking with?" I told him my

name is Tom Bertrand, one of John's assistants. "I know you," he said. "You're the young guy on the video, right?"

I replied, "Yeah, that's me."

Then he said, "I just want to let you know that President Bush is a friend of mine, and although he doesn't have one of your longputters, he's tried mine and borrowed the video to check it out."

I was flattered and couldn't wait to tell John. He didn't seem at all surprised and told me to ship one to the president immediately. As recently as the late 1990s, the now former president was seen still using his longputter.

To market our new phenomenon, we developed elaborate brochures, made a TV commercial, went to golf trade shows, and even carted the longputters around the San Diego Open and the Bob Hope Desert Classic, hoping to get a PGA touring professional to model one. But no such luck. The young Tour players believed that the long sticks were only for seniors who had bad backs and bad nerves. Yet John remained focused and persistent.

On the Monday before the 1989 Shearson Lehman Hutton Open in San Diego (the ninth name change in the tournament's history and its first year since 1967 without the Andy Williams headline), John and I were scouting around the practice green perimeter, looking for someone who would try our longputter. John said that if we hung around with the putter in plain view, one of the pros might give it a try. Other company reps were quietly hustling their various wares around the green.

I was standing with John when I saw Brad Faxon working on his four-footers. After he made three in a row, he glanced around as he waited for Cubby, his caddy for that week, to retrieve the balls from the cup. That's when he spotted me.

I had first met Brad through my Sigma Alpha Epsilon fraternity brothers back in our Furman University days. He had even considered pledging our fraternity but couldn't fit it in with school and golf. I was merely acquainted with Brad back in college but got to know him better when he started playing the Tour in 1984 and made San Diego one of his regular stops. I usually tried to catch up with him during practice rounds or on the range before a tournament round to see if he had any news about our mutual friends.

I looked over at John. He winked at me and said, "Here, tell him to try our putter." He handed me our latest 1.3 model with an offset hosel and leather grips. Like a good soldier, I took the club and leaned it against my body as Brad approached.

"Hey, Bert, how are you?"

"Doing good, Brad. Good to see you again."

John stepped forward and introduced himself. "Hi, Brad, John Schlee."

"Yes, hi, John," Brad replied with recognition in his voice. I had told Brad a couple of years back that I was working with John at his Maximum Golf School.

Without getting further acquainted, John jumped straight to his pitch. "How about giving one of our longputters a try?" John barked like a used car salesman, as he grabbed the longputter and handed it over the gallery rope to Brad, who was well known as one of the best putters on Tour.

Brad fumbled with his hands awkwardly on the grips and politely asked, "How do you use this thing?"

"Let me show you," John said, as he ducked under the rope.

John quickly described various grips and ways to use the pendulum motion with the longputter, as Brad began brushing the club back and forth.

"Why don't you try a few putts with it?" John asked.

"Not today," Brad replied, as he shook his head and handed the putter back to John. "In fact, I've got some things to work on with my own putter. Nice to see you, John, Bert."

And so it went with the touring pros, even those who, unlike Faxon, were always looking for anything that would work to get the ball in the hole.

Several Senior Tour players experimented with our longputters—J. C. Snead, George Archer, Rocky Thompson, Harold Henning, and others. They liked the concept but said that the extra weight inhibited their feel on quick-paced greens. John started looking for alternatives to accommodate the different needs among his Senior Tour connections.

John had an idea that lighter, machine-milled putter heads might do the trick. He contacted Danny Ashcraft, a local scratch golfer and the owner of a computerized milling machine company, to see if he could develop the necessary technology to create John's new designs.

After some hesitation at John's radical ideas, Danny agreed to work on the project. He would do research, supply the raw materials, and create the tooling, while John would supply the designs and the golf connections for marketing. We immediately dropped the casting process and started getting our putter heads milled from blocks of aluminum alloy.

This was a new venture for Danny, and he lost a lot of money on it during the early days, but John got him started in a business that would bring him unimagined success. He recently told me that he has milled more than one million putter heads—more than anyone else in the world—at Western CNC, a company he founded in 1980 in Vista, California. Danny now holds almost thirty worldwide patents on golf clubhead designs. Among his clients are TaylorMade, Callaway, Cobra, and Titleist. His is one of only two companies with contracts to produce the famed Scotty Cameron putters for Titleist. He's also a partner in Hatch Outdoors Co., which produces some of the hottest, high-end fly-fishing reels on the market.

We were having lunch one day when Danny told me an interesting story about Tiger Woods. "Tiger has used the same specially designed Cameron putter to win every single dollar he's made as a professional. When it gets roughed up, Tiger sends it to Scotty, who makes it brand new again. Not long ago, Tiger's wife boxed up his putter to send it in for a tune-up, and she wrote Tiger's name on the return address. There it was, addressed 'From: Tiger Woods . . . To: Scotty Cameron.' He's pretty lucky that package ever got to Scotty."

Tiger's putter would probably set a record on eBay, outdistancing Joe DiMaggio's 56-hit baseball bat or Wayne Gretzky's favorite hockey stick.

Today Danny continues to work closely with Cameron. His latest productions are Titleist's Phantom and Futura putter lines, as well as a new Bull's Eye model.

Meanwhile, John insisted that the new putter heads needed to have some kind of rails. He designed three different sets of brass weights shaped like fat bullets to attach behind the putter face at the heel and toe positions. The threaded weights were easily screwed in and could be changed for optimum performance, depending on the speed of the greens.

The new putter line wasn't finding many takers, but that didn't stop John from trying that much harder. Since most golfers still preferred a standard-length shaft, he also created a shorter model to be sold alongside our long ones.

John was now pouring most of his time and money into the manufacturing end of the business—instead of preparing to join the Senior PGA Tour. His once-thriving Maximum Golf School had become an afterthought. I had been caught up in all the longputter hoopla, but in my heart I really wanted to teach. At Maximum Golf, however, school was out and flatsticks were in.

During those days, I renewed some old friendships in the business world, especially with Bob Vokey and Steve Mata. Vokey went from having a small workshop building and repairing golf clubs in Vista, California, to designing signature wedges for Titleist today. He was the only individual Lee Trevino allowed near his clubs in the early eighties. My friends and I went to Bob to get work done on our clubs many times before he became famous. Mata worked for Vokey in his workshop and later became the top PGA Tour representative for Titleist. Both men worked for TaylorMade back when John and Gary Adams were doing business together.

Maximum Golf longputters remained competitive for about three years, but soon we were eclipsed by the big companies surging into the market with their own designs. One competing model, designed by Dr. Corvi's son, Joe Jr., was very similar to the original Taylor Raylor. We sold about a thousand longputters during this period, but the only professional golfers who used them consistently were Harold Henning and Rocky Thompson on the Senior Tour.

○ ○ ○

Now the time had come for John to jump back on the Tour train and go compete with the seniors. While he was at it, he could promote his longputters, this time from inside the gallery ropes.

3

Maximum Golf:
The Closing Holes

Second Chances

When John reached fifty years of age, he automatically qualified for the Senior Tour, based on money earnings during his twelve-year PGA career. If you had earned enough to be on the top fifty all-time money list, you were in. John's position at number 46 allowed him to bypass the Senior Q-School and the dreaded Monday morning qualifiers. Exemption in hand, John felt confident that he would do well with the Seniors.

In the spring of 1989, shortly before he embarked for his first Senior event, John sat me down and said that the school was now in my hands to do with what I wanted. Advertising had lapsed, and video sales of the teaching system had slowed considerably, but I still wanted to see if I could revive our faltering program.

I ran a few ads to drum up students and conducted my first school with another assistant, Gregg Graham. Expenses ran higher than student fees, however, so I dropped the idea of continuing without John. He *was* the school, and I finally had to accept that it had passed away while we were busy puttering around.

My time was now spent exclusively in the confines of a warehouse, peddling putters to golf shops, while John was out trying to revive his career on the Senior Tour. In his first event in June 1989, he scratched out a couple of 71s in the rain-marred Northville Long Island Classic before stumbling to a final-round 79 and finishing tied for forty-second. His check for $1,750 would be the largest of his Senior Tour career. John played twelve events in his first season, with a scoring average of 76.80, and twenty-four events in 1990, with a scoring average of 76.77.

By the end of 1990, John was ninety-sixth on the Senior money list and never finished higher than forty-second place in all the tournaments he entered. His only Senior round in the 60s was a 66 he shot to tie Gary Player for the first-round lead in the Security Pacific Classic in October 1990. John had scored seven birdies but could only remember making one of them on an 80-foot putt.

"It's hell to get old," he told reporters after the round. "Actually, I have had to concentrate so much on each shot that I just forget what I did."

John was showing signs of forgetting other, more important, things as well. Even though he had overcome the effects of back surgery in 1974 and was in the best shape since his early Tour days, his attention to practice and course management was quickly fading, along with his second chance for fame and glory as a Tour player.

John was getting older but still felt that if he just pushed hard enough and long enough, something good would happen. Success doesn't come simply by pushing for it, however. Hogan had shown John that long hours of intelligent and consistent hard work are the keys to success. But John felt that he was running out of time—time to plan, to practice, to play with care and deliberation. He wanted gratification *now*, and as the months went by, it became apparent that his anxieties had supplanted his hero's work ethic.

As reports of John's dismal showings kept coming back to the office, we all tried to figure out what had changed so radically in the eleven years since he had played with success on the regular Tour. I was pondering this mystery when a clue came to me from a few years earlier.

I had come over to see John at his home office one morning. He had been putting the finishing touches on the manuscript for his *Maximum Golf* book all week, and we were going to review a few points together. I walked into the office and saw Gay sitting silently at her desk. I felt a lot of tension in the room. Then I saw John slouched in his chair at the computer station. He looked like someone had just punched him in the stomach.

"Hey, guys," I said. Gay looked up and smiled but said nothing. John quietly mumbled, "Hey, Tom" as he continued staring at the computer monitor. I glanced toward Gay with a "What's up?" look. She just closed her eyes and slowly shook her head from side to side as if to say, "I'll tell you later." John then got up and, without looking at either of us, said he was going out and would be back later. As John closed the door behind him, Gay went into the kitchen, and a few moments later she left the house. I didn't call after her because something was obviously amiss, and I felt that it was best to let her be.

I walked over to John's computer and noticed a letter on his desk addressed to him from the Ben Hogan company. Not long ago, John had mentioned that he had sent Hogan a letter asking him to write an introduction for the *Maximum Golf* book. The reply had come yesterday, but, strangely enough, it was not signed by Hogan. The gist of the letter was that Hogan wanted nothing to do with the book and that he didn't even remember John Schlee.

I couldn't believe what I'd just read. I could understand Hogan not wanting his name on anyone's book other than his own. He'd said as much before. But he *doesn't remember* John? All those times they'd talked and played together over a period of several years? And what about the prized telegram John received after he won the 1973 Hawaiian Open that said, "ATTABOY. BEN."?

No, that simply couldn't be. I talked to John about it later that week, but he had blown it off (he said, but I wasn't convinced), citing Hogan as a man of mystery.

All I could think of was that someone in the company office had intercepted John's letter and presumed to reply as a way of sheltering, or managing, an aging Hogan. Or, and this came to me later, was Hogan, like John, experiencing the early, unpredictable effects of the Alzheimer's disease that would be instrumental in ending both of their lives?

That was speculating, but not without good reason. I did know that over the past few years, something strange had been evolving in John's world and it showed up in his memory lapses, his attitude, and his performance on the Senior Tour. The thought also occurred to me that Hogan's reply must have cut deeply into John's confidence and enthusiasm. He must have felt abandoned by his master and told himself, in so many words, "Well, if that's the way Hogan feels, to hell with it all." If his words weren't saying it out loud, his actions certainly were.

As well as I had gotten to know John, he didn't talk about his feelings much, and I caught only glimpses of the phantoms of his inner world. Yet I could see that it was becoming a world emptied of hope, while his demons of doubt and despair were gaining ground.

This became painfully evident when I caddied for him at the Gold Rush senior event in Sacramento, California, the last week of October 1990.

I was the only one who knew John's swing inside and out, so I was dispatched by friends and family to see if I could help him out of his continuing funk. John's stepson Jason was his primary caddy during his Senior Tour run, but we agreed that I should get out there and take John's bag during the Gold Rush.

When I arrived, I was completely taken aback as I approached the practice range and saw John hitting balls. He had always been such a perfectionist, a fanatic about filming and studying his swing. Now his alignment had him aimed to the right, and he was overcompensating with his upper body to get the ball in flight toward the target. He was sliding back and forth, overpowering his shots, and they were going everywhere. Even from a distance, he looked flustered and confused.

An eerie sense of foreboding came over me. Who was this guy out there? I'd never seen this version of John before.

It was immediately apparent that John's problems were not strictly from advancing years, from his surgeries, or from thinking too much. They were from thinking too little about what he'd been taught and what he had taught thousands of students. He was out there beating balls like an impatient, hormone-charged kid, while his play was getting progressively worse.

In short, he was ignoring almost every priceless lesson he had learned from the mentor of his youthful dreams, Ben Hogan. I was in a mild state of shock trying to digest all of this as I walked up to John's slot on the practice tee.

"Hey, John."

"Tom, glad you could make it this week," John said with a cheery smile. "And I promise I won't yell at you like I did in Bakersfield."

Ah, yes, Bakersfield. How could I forget my initiation into the ranks as a Tour caddy. Bakersfield was the setting for the second-stage regional qualifier for the PGA Tour in the fall of 1988. As a former Tour player, John had been exempt from the local qualifiers. He figured that this regional competition would be a good tune-up before he joined the Seniors the following summer.

John actually hadn't yelled at me, but he'd had every right to. That had been my first time as a caddy in the big show. I was well versed in the rules of golf, but everything I knew about caddying I'd learned from watching golf tournaments, live and on television.

I was so nervous that on the very first hole of the tournament, I gave John the incorrect yardage to the pin. I felt my heart sink when his perfectly struck ball went screaming past the flag and overshot the green by some ten yards. At first, he gave me a puzzled look, then quickly realized I'd given him the wrong number. He just rolled his eyes and starting walking. We were quiet for a couple of holes, then all was forgotten while I paid much closer attention to my calculations.

Now here we were on the Senior Tour, and, despite John's reassuring words, I sent up a little prayer that both of us would turn in a better job performance this time around.

"I've been having a little trouble lining up lately," John said. "Can you take a look?"

"Sure." I moved over behind him as he aimed toward a tree

in the distance. "You're set up pretty far to the right," I said confidently.

"Really?" John sounded surprised.

"Let me show you, but hold still. Don't move," I said, as I ran over to his bag, grabbed one of his clubs, and set it down behind his heels. He stepped away from the ball and stood right next to me, eyeing where the club was pointing down range.

"Wow, I wonder how I got so goofed up?" John said, as he walked back and adjusted his setup position. He meticulously set his feet, looked back to me, and asked, "How's that?"

I smiled and said, "Perfect." All right, I thought, so far so good.

After I helped straighten out his alignment and lower-body turn toward the target, he began swinging well on the driving range. In fact, if you would have gone up and down the line and watched his fellow competitors, you probably would have picked him to finish in the top ten.

○ ○ ○

John's troubles began the moment he teed off on the first hole of the tournament.

The first hole was about 380 yards and straight away on a gradual downhill slope to the green. I stood by the bag, and John pulled out his driver. I said to myself, "What is he thinking?" This hole puts a premium on accuracy and does nothing for a long hitter because the fairway ends at about 280 yards, followed by thick rough through to the green. In the practice rounds, John had been pounding many of his drives well past the 300-yard mark. I just held my breath and waited for the inevitable.

John addressed the ball swiftly and calmly crushed it. I knew it would outrun the fairway the moment it cracked off his clubface. It landed well into the thick rough and stopped about 75 yards from the green without a prayer. He hacked it up on the green to about 45 feet from the hole and two-putted for his par.

I was screaming inside, "Hogan wouldn't have liked the way you just played that hole!" I couldn't say anything out loud because in the practice round John had told me, in a matter-of-fact manner, that he would make his club selections, and, unless he asked for my opinion, my job was to haul the bag, figure yardage, and otherwise be quiet and watch the show.

John came back with a couple of birdies and the leader board showed us at two under after five holes. But then he made a pair of double bogeys, and everything went south from there. On the eighth, a par 5, John's drive came to rest in the woods off to the right. When I realized where the ball had landed, I could see no safe play to the green. The lie was okay, but the ball sat behind a group of trees so thick we couldn't see the green. We had already lost four strokes in the last two holes, and this was not the time to gamble.

John demanded, "Gimme the 4-wood." I brought the bag over to him, amazed at the bewildered look on his face. Gone was the air of self-assurance, the composure of a seasoned professional that he'd shown on the first tee. Now he was deep in a cloud of chaotic, stressed-out panic. No player in his right mind would try to escape this predicament with a wood. Even most weekend amateurs know that when you're in trouble, you first get the ball back in play, then take your lumps and make the best of it.

John took a half-hearted practice swing and set up to the ball. The ensuing swing was powerful and graceful, but the ball exploded high off the clubface, smacked an overhanging limb, and raced out of bounds.

Before I could digest what had just happened, I heard, "Gimme another ball." I guess I didn't move fast enough, because he barked, "Come on, hurry up!" I quickly tossed him another ball, and at that instant I flashed back to a day gone by during an outside session at one of our schools.

We had gathered the students around John to watch him execute some golf shots that we'd discussed in the classroom. He captivated his audience with controlled fades and draws, hitting them high and low. I tossed him a ball for each shot, a routine we'd done many times before. After I lobbed him about six balls, he quipped, in a testy tone for everyone to hear, "What do I look like, some monkey in a zoo? You're tossing me balls like they're peanuts. Just set me a pile over here and pay attention."

I was surprised by his sudden irritation and quickly dumped a small bucket on the range mat, then stepped aside. Some students were sneaking quizzical glances at me. I looked back at them, as surprised as they were, and just shrugged my shoulders.

Later that afternoon when our students were busy hitting balls, I went to John and apologized for making him feel like an animal in a zoo. He laughed and said, "Tom, I didn't mean to jump on you like that, but it suddenly reminded me of the days on Tour. When you think about it, that's what we were, animals in a traveling zoo, putting on a show. We were on display for all to come and see us do things with a golf ball that most people can't do. Twelve years on the road show can get you feeling pretty calloused, and sometimes you just snap."

John elaborated with a story. "One time I was playing early on a Thursday morning, and there weren't a lot of people around watching. I was on a par three on the front nine, my ball teed up closer to the right tee marker, and some guy from the gallery comes right up to the rope and starts spouting how he wants to see me play this hole with a nice little draw. I think it was in Chicago for the 1968 Western Open. Anyway, I smile and go into my setup routine and this guy can't keep his feet still. I stop, moving only my head up to look at the guy, and he says, 'Aren't you going to swing at it?'

"All I could think of was, I'm out here trying to make a living and I'm supposed to put up with this? I put my head back down, took two steps and a hop. Next thing I knew I swept my 5-iron back and came down hard, right on top of the tee marker. Wood splintered everywhere, and the man with the smart mouth took off running.

"As if nothing had happened, I went right back to my setup, with a little chuckling from my playing partners. My 5-iron was fine, and I never did hear anything from the officials, but the tight little fade I hit set me up for my first birdie of the day."

John wasn't going to birdie *this* hole today, when in reality he should have had a good shot at one. He was hitting four, and he swung the 4-wood again. This time, he got it out of the woods and into the greenside rough on his way to making a 7. This travesty continued until the end of the round and a final score of 78, after starting with a couple early birdies.

I was in shock. What happened to playing for the landing areas? Or taking what the course gives on a particular day? What happened to everything Hogan had taught John? Now he was charging at the course like a weekend hack. My stomach was churning.

We went to the range after the round, and he immediately reached for the driver. It was a replica of the blonde-headed driver John Daly had made famous after he won the PGA Championship. Made of some space-age material, it was designed for "gaining those extra yards." Like John needed extra yards. So why practice the driver? On this course, you needed a driver four times, maybe five.

As he launched ball after ball almost to the end of the range, a grin replaced the scowl he'd worn when he walked off 18. This was the grin he'd had on hole 14 where they measure your driving distance. John had blasted a monster drive low and to the left side of the fairway, 307 yards against the wind. "Good one, John," said one of his playing partners, Julius Boros. John was beaming. Not bad for someone who's fifty years old, I had to admit.

Now, as I looked around the practice tee, I could see other players checking out John's booming drives.

"I hit that last one a little thin," he remarked to no one in particular, as he delicately set another ball on a tee, his pinky finger pointing to the sky.

He stood there pummeling balls with his driver for about forty minutes. The only other club he took out of the bag was the sand wedge. He hit it three times, and that ended the practice session.

That evening John's wife joined us for dinner in the clubhouse dining room. Shortly after we ordered, I couldn't hold back any longer.

"John, why did you hit your driver off the first tee when you know you can set yourself up better with a 3-iron?"

Gay glanced in my direction. She understood what I was doing, smiled, and looked at John. He put down his soup spoon and wiped his chin. Feeling the heat of my gaze and the interest from Gay, he countered, "What are you saying? You think I'm playing too aggressive?"

The hairs on the back of my neck were tingling. It wasn't easy looking at him when his eyes grew hard, which usually signaled an explosion or a caustic response. I persisted. "You always told me Hogan said to play the golf course and not let the golf course play you. You seem to be trying to overpower the course, and I think it's getting you into trouble."

I looked over at Gay, and she took it as her cue to say something. "You were in trouble an awful lot today, John," she said, as she settled her hands around her drink.

John looked at both of us. "I don't think hitting a 3-iron off the first tee would have helped my game today, but I tell you what, I'll hit a 3-iron tomorrow and we'll see what happens."

"Great!" I exclaimed, immensely relieved. "Tomorrow's going to be just great."

I couldn't believe he was being so cooperative, considering that I had directly questioned his ability to think on the golf course. At the same time, I felt sort of infantile, like a kid who'd expected a parental thrashing but got a piece of candy instead.

When I arrived at the course early the next morning, I was struck by how peaceful and serene it appeared. The rich, thick scent of newly mown grass and the fragrance of awakening wildflowers made me stop and drink in several deep breaths. The rising sun shot its rays through the trees and sparkled in the morning dew. What a beautiful setting, so calm and bright—until the intensity of competition would brush it all aside. A hazy thought passed through my mind about how far this old shepherd's game had drifted away from the simple pleasures of nature.

My attention jumped back to the business at hand. I had been persuaded to come to this event to influence John and his outcome in the tournament. Speaking up as I did the night before was part of my function for being here. I felt a sense of accomplishment, a deed well done. Now we'd find out whether my advice had landed in fertile soil or on the rocks.

I met John outside the locker room, and we headed for the practice tee. I knew he wouldn't spend much time there. Typically, he would hit sixteen to twenty-four shots before a tournament round and finish with one of his favorite remarks: "It doesn't take much to warm up a Rolls Royce." He appeared to be his confident old self today, wide awake and in a bright mood.

We ambled over to the practice green, where John ran through his brief preround putting routine, then went back to the locker room. His tee time was approaching ever so slowly, and I was itching to see him hit his drive with the 3-iron. I looped up the bag and walked over to the first tee to watch a few players tee off. They all hit drivers.

Would John even remember that he'd told me he would hit the 3-iron? Nothing was mentioned on the practice range, but not much is said there anyway. What if he asked for the bag and started to pull out the driver? Would I stop him? In front of everybody?

My mind was a racetrack full of hounds chasing the pace-car rabbit. I had a strong feeling that there was way more at stake here than which club he'd use off the first tee. I believed we were standing at a crossroads, that this was one of those rare moments when one's destiny is decided. Everything was on the line, and John was about to choose an irreversible path to his future. His driver was pointing down one road, his 3-iron pointing down the other.

Would John come back to everything he had learned and revered during his days with Hogan? Or would he thrash onward in his present course like a frustrated hacker whose only consolation was hitting big drives, while his dream fell apart in front of him and everyone else?

At the same time, I chastised myself for overdramatizing the whole situation, especially my part in it. What's the big deal anyway? John is having a bad day, a bad year. But the truth swept all that aside and I knew I was witnessing a man and his dreams on the threshold of an agonizing death. He was entering the November of his years, and he desperately wanted it to be April again.

I turned to look for him. We were due on the tee, where the other two players and caddies had already assembled. I picked up the bag and started to lift the yellow gallery rope, when John seemed to appear out of nowhere to give me a hand.

"Ready for some fun?" he asked, as I hoisted the bag into position behind the right tee marker.

"I sure am," I replied, relieved that he was there and we could get this round underway. "This course owes us a little something extra today," I said, referring to some bad bounces we'd had in yesterday's round. I had already decided that when it was his turn to tee off, I would keep my hands over the cover of the driver.

His two playing partners, Joe Jimenez and Jerry Barber, hit their drivers, and then it was John's turn. "Next up on the first tee, from Carlsbad, California, John Schlee," announced the tournament official.

John smiled and tipped his visor to the small gathering of fans as they politely applauded. He made his way over to me, and before I knew what he was doing, he had the 3-iron in his hands and started slow, smooth practice swings. I could hardly contain my joy as the marshals began quieting the crowd. If they only knew what I was going through to persuade this man on the tee to play the course with some finesse, the way he'd taught his students to play for so many years.

John went through his deliberate setup routine, settled the club behind the ball, and swung away. The swing looked solid and the finish balanced, but he blocked it right, and the ball found a fairway bunker about 235 yards off the tee.

John's mood completely changed. A dark cloud formed under the brim of his visor that hooded his eyes, and his features furrowed with anger. When he approached the bag, I was gazing down the fairway toward the bunker, trying to figure a preliminary yardage to the pin. Truthfully, I couldn't bear to look him in the face.

"See what happens when I hit an iron off the tee!" He glowered at me as he thrust the 3-iron into my hand so hard it banged my knuckles. Then he turned and strode quickly down the fairway.

It was like a slap in the face. I picked up the bag and scooted after him, trying to disentangle my earlier optimism from the dreaded gloom that descended on both of us. Was it my fault he blocked it into the sand? Should I keep my mouth shut from now on when it comes to his play? Would I be just another excuse for a poor score?

John ended up making bogey and I ended up speaking only when spoken to for the remainder of that day and the remainder of that weekend. His last two rounds of 86–73 left him at the bottom of the field, but it didn't seem to matter. John would travel to another event the following week, where he could be king of the range once again.

On the plane homeward, I couldn't help feeling sorry for John. He hadn't made good showings for his students around the country, and he hadn't followed a professional plan to attack his tournament battlefields intelligently. Most disturbing of all, he was playing as if he'd never even heard of Hogan.

I was spent, more dispirited than anything. I'd thought I could make a difference by giving him some needed help as his swing coach. At first he had listened, and part of his old professional persona resurfaced, but it didn't seem to register for very long. Something else was taking its place.

As I gazed out the plane's window, watching the hills and ribbons of roadways drift below us, I realized that I was quickly losing interest in Maximum Golf and John Schlee. At that moment, I saw him as a man who had abandoned his dreams and was dragging mine down with them on a rapid descent into his personal hell.

Now I often look back and suspect that the early symptoms of John's Alzheimer's disease were evident on the practice range and during the Gold Rush rounds. Maybe they'd even begun months or years earlier and had steadily gnawed at him all that time. His decisions had become increasingly muddled and irrational. His practice and play seemed defiant and contentious, like a condemned man whose anger was the only antidote to despair that he could summon.

Some dark force was tearing at John's soul and killing his game, and neither of us understood what it was at the time.

At the End of the Day

I went back to work Monday with a different attitude about Maximum Golf, the company, and my passion for the last several years. I was certain that I didn't belong there anymore, and I began to look for a graceful and honorable way out. Yet I felt held in place by the powerful inertia of all the exciting years I'd spent there as a student, a teacher, a dreamer—and by a nebulous hope that maybe some miracle would turn things around. Yet it wasn't destined to be so, and the next seven months would be a tortuous affair.

John wasn't playing as much on Tour because expenses were far more than the token $500 he earned for showing up and finishing near the bottom. He spent almost every day working in the machine shop, trying to come up with a new putter design that TaylorMade might be interested in. Incoming calls were rare in those days, but the company continued to telemarket its current stock of putters to golf pro shops with limited success.

By the end of May 1991, Gay had become concerned about their financial situation. She whisked into the office one day and informed me rather abruptly that I would assume the duties of telemarketer and that we needed to jump on it right now. But I'd had enough. I told her in so many words that I could not and would not and that I quit. I had a nineteen-month-old daughter to support and felt that I had to get away from this whole desperate affair, get back to some kind of productive reality. I walked out of the office and never turned back.

I didn't see or talk to John for a long time after that day. He had known I was frustrated but had been willing to stay with him for a few months in some vain hope that things would change for the better. Meanwhile, he kept fiddling with his putters, while our old teaching business faded into distant memories.

Now he was losing me, his trusty right-hand man, along with many others who had been caught up in his dreams. Gregg, Lin, and Bruce were pursuing other interests and rarely dropped by anymore. John was preoccupied with new dreams, and, strangest of all, he didn't seem to care who was around to share them with.

Crazy as it was at times, John had always been sincerely concerned about everyone who worked with him. We were his support team, and he appreciated that we all helped to keep things cooking at Maximum Golf. He took good care of his troops, while we enjoyed a wonderful ride financially, socially, and professionally. We believed in him, and he had never let us down until lately, when it became evident that some mysterious force was taking him down.

I heard from John only once more, about three years after I'd left. I was at home playing with my son in the family room when the phone rang. "Hello," I said, still making faces at my son across the room.

"Tom, John Schlee here. How's it going?"

A smile spread across my face. Remembering all the good times we had, I said, "Fine, John, and how about you?"

John always got right to the point. "Well, I've been doing some teaching and was thinking of starting up the golf school again. Lin Wicks and I thought you might be interested. What do you say?"

My mind wandered over the previous three years and how I couldn't seem to break in *anywhere* in the golf business. I couldn't get a job teaching because I wasn't in the PGA, and I couldn't get a job in the manufacturing end except as a minimum-wage club assembler. I had returned to the restaurant business to support my family, which now included my soul mate, Heidi; her daughter, Taylor; my daughter, Lindsey; and our son, Logan. I couldn't stake their future on another of John's whims. I felt as if I'd be going backward if I accepted his offer.

So I said, "Sorry, John, I'm done with golf. Got to look after my family now." We talked for a few minutes about life and golf.

I didn't let on that I knew he and Gay were no longer together. When I hung up the phone, I knew that I probably would never talk with him again, and a wave of relief and sadness came over me. I made a promise to myself, then and there, that somehow, on my own terms, I would teach again by the time I was fifty.

Within months of our phone conversation, John became incapacitated by the effects of Alzheimer's disease.

I ran into Gay every now and then at Capriccio's Salon in Carlsbad. She had started doing hair again after she and John parted ways. Many times we asked each other, "Have you heard anything about John?" and the answer was always, "No." My old teaching partners, Gregg Graham and Lin Wicks, were the only ones who occasionally checked in with John, and I hadn't been in touch with them for a while.

Lin later told me that John had been living with him and his wife, occasionally teaching at Pleasant Valley C.C. in the Portland area and Monterey Peninsula C.C. in Carmel. Then, when John was finally diagnosed with Alzheimer's, he moved back with his parents for a time. When they could no longer care for him, they put him in an assisted-living facility sometime during the winter of 1994–1995. A short time later, they institutionalized him with the state of California.

I got a call from Gregg, out of the blue, in the winter of 2000. He said that John wasn't doing so well these days and would I be interested in seeing him? "Yes, definitely," I replied. We arranged to meet just outside the state hospital where John was staying so Gregg could brief me on what I was about to see. John had become obese during his initial stay, weighing in excess of 250 pounds at one point, but now he was extremely thin. Gregg said that John couldn't speak any longer and made only irregular sounds that he could no longer shape into words.

I don't know if anyone is ever prepared to see another human being who was once so vibrant and full of life now appear like a skeleton restrained to his bed. The moment I walked into John's hospital room, his eyes rarely left my face. I searched his face, too, then couldn't avoid noticing the white tube socks pulled halfway up his bony shins and the loose-fitting hospital gown draping over his emaciated 90-pound body.

John was trying to move about and making muffled sounds as if he wanted to say something to me. His eyes were wild and frightening, flashing around as he struggled in vain to break out of this awful nightmare, with no doors or windows in sight. I was thankful I hadn't brought any members of my family with me.

"Hi, John. It's me, Tom Bertrand," I said, not knowing whether he could hear or even understand me. Yet somehow I thought he could. As I stood there, John glanced at Gregg as if asking, "Is that Tom?" and then looked back at me, grunting and shifting around as if trying to show or tell me something. My heart sank in despair for this man, my old teacher and mentor, and an awful taste rose into my mouth.

Here was a once-vibrant being who had always been busy creating something, his high-speed mind working overtime, never satisfied with what was and always looking for a better way. Now he lay there completely helpless, unable to speak or get out of bed, visibly grappling with the invisible demons of his disease.

Right then, I flashed back to the past: the schools we'd experienced, the golf we'd played, the fun and exciting times we'd had, and the knowledge that had passed from Hogan through John to me and that I now held in my care like a sacred scroll. All the old frustrations had long been forgiven and forgotten, and I wished desperately that things could have turned out differently for John.

I stood in the room for about ten minutes, telling John how glad I was to be there and how I hoped he was being cared for properly. I started to stammer, wondering what else I could say, when Gregg said we should go.

I turned to look at John one last time. He was watching me with a troubled, searching look in his eyes. My eyes welled up as I offered a silent prayer for him. Then I said good-bye and walked away.

Gregg and I stood in the parking lot and talked for a while about the old times and how fate had dealt John this hard final hand. No matter what John had become, we would remember him as the golf teacher ahead of his time, a dynamic character who gave his all to whatever dream won his attention, a natural optimist who kept getting back up and couldn't wait to take another run at it, and an unpredictable maverick who could warm your heart or make you feel like crawling in a hole.

John had pioneered the longputter, the interchangeable weighting system to adjust clubhead balance that's so in vogue today, and several innovative teaching aids. He'd been a charter member of the renaissance in golf club manufacturing that gave birth to the metalwood revolution and custom-milled putters. He had trekked the Olympian heights of the PGA Tour and languished near the bottom of the Senior Tour. He was among the few professionals whose physical conditioning and brand of power golf previewed the aggressive style of today's young Tour tigers.

Through it all, John was always grateful for the little morsels of fame that fate kicked his way, even a small scramble tournament his team had won in 1986.

When John was asked if he had played any competitive golf

during the decade between his PGA days and the Senior Tour, he replied with enthusiasm, "Oh, yes, there was the Dooley McCluskey Invitational in Carlsbad." (Dooley's was the restaurant I worked at before joining John's school full time, and this was the tournament I continued to organize every year for a bunch of local players.)

"My team won," John said proudly, "and I got free lunch and dinner at his restaurant for a year. That's not to be sneezed at."

○ ○ ○

On my drive home from the hospital, I made up my mind that I would finish the book on instruction that John and I had started back in his office in Carlsbad. Circumstances had delayed the work, but my mission remained as clear as day. I didn't know when or how I would do it, but I vowed to make it happen.

I felt as if I were floating down the freeway, thinking about John, as my mind wandered through the times we'd experienced, our hopes and dreams. Then one clear scene settled into view that seemed to capture the essence of John's journey through life.

He was sitting across from me in his living room on a Sunday night. We were sipping a glass of chardonnay and enjoying a long, slow exhale after one of our three-day golf schools. Our conversation turned to the time he had shared the lead in the 1973 U.S. Open and had trouble sleeping the night before the final round.

"Tom, you should have seen me. Normally, I like to stay up late when I have a late tee time the following day, so I can stay in bed longer. That way, I don't worry about finding things to do for six hours or more before I tee off."

His mind was now fully back in Oakmont; I could see it in his eyes.

"I think I stared at the ceiling all night Saturday," John said with a chuckle. "When I got to the course the next morning, I was like a thoroughbred itching to run, but I had to wait and then wait some more." He sat for a moment with a relaxed, distant look on his face. Then he put down his wine glass, stood up, and went into his setup procedure as he gripped an imaginary club.

"Playing in the last group of any tournament is exciting, but nothing is more exciting than being in the last group on a Sunday, in a major championship, and having a chance to win." John's eyes were sparkling now, completely caught up in his reverie as he waggled his invisible club. He was right there on the first tee, paired with Arnold Palmer, several groups behind Johnny Miller, who would come from six shots back that day with a 63, leaving John one stroke short of a playoff.

"So many people were packed around the first tee," John continued. "I tried not to notice, to stay focused on my shot at hand."

Here in the living room, he moved into his unique impact address position, swung the imaginary club back, and then whipped it through to a full finish. He held his finishing pose a moment, watching his shot.

"When I made contact, I knew I'd blocked it and wouldn't like the result," John continued. "I was told it might be out of bounds, so I hit a provisional. I found my first drive inbounds, but it was lodged in a bush, unplayable, and even with relief I still couldn't swing at the ball. Of course, that took my provisional ball out of play, and I had to make the long walk back to hit another.

"It was so strange going back to the first tee. Hundreds of people were watching us tee off only moments ago, but now the only person in sight was an older gentleman in coveralls. He was holding a bag and a pole with a nail in the end, poking around picking up discarded cups and wrappers.

"When the old man saw me walk up, he stopped poking and stared at me with a questioning look on his face. Then he said, 'Not so good, huh?'

"'No, not so good,' I said, as I teed up a new ball. 'But wait'll you see this next shot.'"

John went on to double bogey the first hole and came right back with an eagle on the fourth. He managed to shoot 70 for the day and 280 for the tournament, one ahead of Weiskopf and two ahead of Palmer, Nicklaus, and Trevino. Of the seventy-three previous U.S. Opens, John's final score would have won sixty-three of them.

○ ○ ○

In early July 2000, I was getting my hair cut in Gay's salon, when she came over and told me that John had passed away the previous month. Immediately I felt sorrow, but it quickly turned to relief and peace because I knew that his miserable condition would no longer keep him a prisoner in this world.

John died on his sixty-first birthday, alone in his room and without a penny to his name. Because of the long struggle with his affliction, he was completely unaware that Hogan had passed away three years before him.

Gregg called some time later to tell me that he had spread John's ashes around a little spruce tree he had planted in the Idyllwild area above Palm Springs. He and John had hiked up to that spot a couple of times. John enjoyed its broad vistas and the scent of pines and crisp mountain air, a nice respite from the hectic pace of his normal world. It is a perfect garden for his earthly remains.

John Schlee's creative, tumultuous spirit has a special place in the heart of everyone who knew him, especially me. He invited me in to an ideal home where my dreams could flourish, where I could practice my passion and study the best in the business with kindred spirits. His unfiltered "go for it" style will always be an inspiration. He gave me a gift of knowledge that I could have found nowhere else unless Ben Hogan himself had personally taken me under his wing.

I'll always smile when I think of that guy who barged in on me one day long ago at the Olympic driving range. He turned me inside out and around, gave me some truth and made me like it. Then he assured me, as he walked off, that I'd "eventually get it."

Thank you, John. I got it. And now it belongs to everyone.

4

Tracking the Secret

A note from the authors: We searched everywhere for a complete chronological summary of when and how Hogan disclosed the many aspects of the secret he first mentioned almost seventy years ago and the impact that each revelation made on the golfing world. Bits and pieces of information were scattered everywhere, but we found nothing that collects all the main facts and observations into one place to give us an overview of its development. We also conducted street polls of average golfers and found a rash of misconceptions and huge gaps in awareness about Hogan—his secrets, his contributions to the art of the golf swing, and his record. So we figured that we'd better dig in and compile this retrospective ourselves. It's the first time, we believe, that anything like this has been done. What follows is a survey of the birth and development of Hogan's secret, along with decade-by-decade highlights of its evolution to the present day.

○ ○ ○

By the late 1940s, Ben Hogan's approach shots were hitting so many flag sticks—and bouncing away far from the cup—that he changed his target from the hole itself to a few feet below it. He had discovered ways to translate his dreaded hook into a consistent power fade. His machinelike swing, hard earned during thousands of hours of steady grinding on the practice range, was finally putting trophies on his shelf and welcome dollars in his pocket.

From 1946 until his devastating car accident in 1949, Hogan won thirty-seven tournaments—eleven of the last sixteen events he entered—including two PGAs and a U.S. Open. He captured the money title in five of the seven seasons he played in that decade, with time out for a tour of duty with the U.S. Army Air Corps during World War II.

What looked like the end of his career in 1949 actually marked the beginning of one of the most inspiring resurrections in the history of sports. With his meticulously crafted golf game and a monumental will like few before or since, Hogan compelled his maimed body to perform the feats of legends. His astounding comeback in 1950 produced six more majors, culminating in his Triple Crown (Masters, U.S. Open, British Open) in 1953.

As with other heroes before him, the results of Hogan's single-minded dedication to his goal appeared to many as the work of magic. For the rest of his life and thereafter, the public would be mystified, often confused, and never quite satisfied in its relentless search for the secrets of his success.

A bemused Hogan, meanwhile, knew that his growing mastery was the child of a burning passion focused by a considerable amount of intelligence consistently applied to a prodigious

amount of work. The golf gods must respond to such rare determination, and throughout Hogan's career, they dispensed timely
guidance and insights upon their protégé as he toiled in the dirt
below.

Even so, the work didn't come easy. Hogan's dream of
becoming a successful professional golfer came to life only after
a long, frustrating journey. Along with Byron Nelson and many
other players, Hogan had picked up the game in the caddy ranks
during the 1920s. In 1929, at the age of seventeen, he set out on
the fledgling player's tour but didn't win his first paycheck, a tidy
$8.50, until the L.A. Open in 1932.

Long hours of continuous practice steadily refined his game,
yet he found spotty success on Tour. For the next decade and a
half, he wrestled mightily with a confounding tendency to hook
his shots, especially the driver. Too often, he had been poised to
win a tournament only to see his hopes snapped away into the
woods.

What then seemed an unshakable curse that almost drove
him from the game would ultimately prove to be the blessing of
a lifetime. In his obsession to find a cure for his hook, he worked
ceaselessly until he fashioned what few can dispute is *the* most
effective and repeatable golf swing in the sport's five-hundred-
year history. He searched for a solution and found immortality.

As Hogan began winning tournaments in the early 1940s,
players and fans took notice of his new success story. Why is
Hogan suddenly making acceptance speeches after more than a
decade as a struggling hopeful? Yet their questions about his
growing success met with Hogan's impenetrable gaze and polite
but cryptic comments. Few people realized that Hogan's genuine
modesty and shyness made him very uncomfortable talking
about himself. He was a discreet Texas gentleman in all respects,

but his natural reticence was often perceived as aloofness, even arrogance.

Fellow players began to suspect that Hogan had discovered a vein of golf gold and selfishly wanted to keep it all for himself. The sportswriters were curious, too, and soon a buzz was going around that Hogan had a secret, a magic pill that, if you could discover and digest it, would explain all and revolutionize your game.

But Hogan wasn't talking.

Soon "a secret" became "*the* secret," while Hogan's continued silence and success only fueled the public's growing demand to know.

From Hogan's point of view, he was just a player laboring away on his golf game while everyone else was looking for secret formulas encoded somewhere inside the fruits of those labors. Hogan began telling his inquisitors that they had to "dig it out of the dirt" as he had. The magic is in the work, he implied, and that's no secret.

At the time, his advice was as novel as it was profound, because in those days most Tour players did little more than a few warm-up swings between tournaments. Hogan's earthy axiom was far too homespun to satisfy the public's thirst for a more exotic explanation. Besides, that would mean more work if you wanted to improve your game—an acceptable alternative only if all else failed.

The notion of a tell-all secret, however, wasn't entirely fermented in the public mind. In fairness to the golf paparazzi of the time and their lust for hot quotes and epiphanies, Hogan did discreetly remark to his pal Jimmy Demaret as early as 1937, "I've got the secret of this game now." Yet his record for the next few years spoke otherwise. As with so many fleeting insights, whatever the technique was worked well on the range, only to fall apart in the heat of competition.

Then in 1940, Hogan started winning, and winning changes everything.

Hogan had also begun to understand the value of his hard-won accomplishments. Although he seldom, if ever, mentioned it, he must have been intrigued by the possibility of cashing in on his rarest of commodities, a golf game that could win professional tournaments. You could almost hear him thinking, If the public wants to call it a secret, I can give 'em one—when I'm ready, and for a price. Those were the days of the Tour's infancy, when sponsors, agents, and lucrative endorsements were as rare as double-eagles. To survive, you had to create your own extra cash flow to supplement the meager purses of the day.

By the time of his head-on collision with a Greyhound bus in 1949, Hogan had become the dominant force in professional golf, often beating a tough field that included Byron Nelson, Sam Snead, Gene Sarazen, Jimmy Demaret, and other solid players. He had developed the near-perfect, choke-proof golf swing and was burning it into his cellular memory through endless hours of practice, rarely missing a single day on the practice range.

Now he would miss at least a year—maybe a lifetime—of competition while his crushed bones healed, and he slowly learned to stand and walk again. Doctors told him that the likelihood of his ever again using his wrecked body to play golf ranged from extremely remote to impossible. He would be in constant pain the rest of his life.

Yet he soon returned with even greater force to begin one of the most phenomenal recoveries of all time in any field of endeavor. Within eleven months of being pulled half-dead from the wreckage, he tied Snead in the L.A. Open, then lost in the 18-hole playoff. Five months later, he won the 1950 U.S. Open at Merion. For the next three years, he continued his miraculous streak, winning two more U.S. Opens, two Masters, and his only entry to the British Open at Carnoustie, the final jewel in his legendary Triple Crown.

On his return from Scotland, Hogan rode in a hero's ticker-tape parade down Broadway as his hero Bobby Jones had before. Hogan had become the Tiger Woods of his day and an archetype of willpower and determination for the ages.

Now the buzz about "the secret" swelled into a persistent clamor that made headlines here and across the Atlantic. Everyone was asking, How could a permanently crippled man, whose every step caused excruciating pain, now play a better game than he did *before* his accident? How could anyone emerge from his near-deathbed and win six major golf tournaments in four years? This indeed was incredible, magical.

It was almost like following Babe Ruth's sixty-homer binge or Jesse Owens plucking Olympic gold in the Nazis' backyard or Bobby Jones's "Impregnable Quadrilateral"—with one crucial exception. Those feats were accomplished by healthy men, while Hogan reached his pinnacle in agonizing pain and barely able to walk. In the public's mind, only divine intervention or a powerful secret formula could explain the miracle of Hogan's comeback.

Some of Hogan's fellow competitors, themselves beginning to experience the fruits of hard work, were miffed by all the hoopla about this so-called "secret." An amused Hogan understood their envy for what it was: a thinly veiled desire to learn for free what had cost him years to attain.

During those early touring days, when players traveled and ate and drank together, few secrets survived the repartee of the

19th hole. Yet if you'd figured out some way to have an edge and increase your chances of making a paycheck, you didn't talk it up at the bar, especially if you were Ben Hogan. You quietly put it to work so you could get your best share of the small purses offered in the pre-TV days of professional golf.

Shortly before he retired from serious competition following the 1955 U.S. Open, Hogan made a deal with *Life* magazine that he'd tell all for a sum of $10,000. They broke the story, titled "This Is My Secret," in August 1955, and magazine sales went off the charts. While many people were satisfied to at last read about, if not understand, the proffered keys to Hogan's success, the article also sparked a new round of speculation and analysis. Some players thought he was still holding out crucial information. Some claimed he was putting everybody on and did it just for the money. Others, among them John Schlee, took Hogan's gold and went to work.

In 1957, Hogan released his landmark book *Five Lessons: The Modern Fundamentals of Golf*, in which he outlines, with customary workmanship and modesty, the essentials of a good golf swing. It's as if he piled in front of us all the gems he had mined during his three decades of solitude and practice. In his eyes, the secret is still in the work, in the dirt. This classic book continues to be one of the all-time best sellers in any sport and in any field.

Time-Life, Inc.'s hot new publication *Sports Illustrated* ran a five-part series on the book before it came out. Without Hogan's authorization, *SI* had previously run some of the 1955 *Life* photos in a spin-off piece, then reportedly agreed to pay an outraged Hogan $20,000 in recompense.

Besides Hogan himself, James Dodson, in his excellent biography *Ben Hogan: An American Life*, closes in on the roots of the secret: "His real secret lay not in the technical jargon of some fractional manipulation of the glide path of the club at impact . . . but rather in the rarest combination of an extraordinarily disciplined brain and an undeniable will power fueled by a fierce survival instinct to prevail against all odds." As in the movie *Field of Dreams*, build such a power center and the details will come.

Thus the search continued on through Hogan's lifetime and, as the following chronology of highlights shows, thereafter to this day. Now the complete and final revelations of Hogan's secret, assembled in the following pages of this book, may at last mark the end of more than half a century of speculation and confusion as to what makes Ben Hogan the benchmark of golf swings and an enduring model of the classic self-made master.

For now, let's briefly review the origins and development of Hogan's secret from the first tee to the final hole. Here we summarize Hogan's comments, along with impressions from touring pros, instructors, sportswriters, and other aficionados on the many facets of this enduring, prismatic golf mystery.

o o o

1930s

After turning pro in 1929, Ben Hogan makes several failed attempts to earn his living on the professional circuit during the first half of the decade. In a 1983 interview with Ken Venturi on CBS, Hogan recalls the old days and explains his game in these words: "I was always last if I got in the money at all. As I said, I was a terrible player."

The search is on for a durable, precision golf game, which will give birth to Hogan's secrets. Hogan has a severe hooking problem that he likes to describe as "a low, ducking, agonizing hook, the kind you could hang your coat on. When it caught the rough, it was the terror of the field mice." Even with this terrible flaw, by the end of the decade he is able to make expenses and a modest living playing the Tour.

In 1939, Henry Picard, Hogan's Tour mentor and friend, advises a weaker grip (move the left hand until the thumb is more on top of the shaft, rather than to the right as in a "strong" grip) and a more open stance to help resolve the hooking problem. The new grip immediately begins to straighten out Hogan's tee shots. An immensely relieved Hogan believes he is "onto something big" now, and he later credits this change as part of his secret.

○ ○ ○

1940s
Hogan is winning golf tournaments and becomes the Tour's leading money winner in 1940, 1941, and 1942, mainly because his putting improves, but he still struggles to incorporate the new "weaker" grip. He gradually reverts to a stronger grip, and his nemesis hook surfaces yet again. He misses three seasons on the Tour when he joins the U.S. Army Air Corps and serves until the end of World War II.

In the spring of 1946, the wartime layoff finds a discouraged Hogan leaving the Tour and heading home to Fort Worth, Texas, desperate to find a permanent solution to his hooking crisis. He leaves his clubs in the bag and spends a few days pondering his impasse, until one night the blueprint of a profound revelation takes shape in his mind. His inspiration comes in the form of two keys he will keep tucked out of sight until the 1955 *Life* magazine story (see "1950s").

With a newly revived game, Hogan again takes the money title in 1946 and 1948. He wins the 1948 U.S. Open and the PGA. He discreetly lets it be known to a few close friends that he is working on something, but doesn't say what it is. He has unearthed several secrets by now, and the public is clamoring for whatever he's willing to hand out. Near the end of this decade, he is the dominant force on Tour with 37 victories, including three majors. Then in 1949, Hogan's car accident almost ends his life and certainly, doctors believe, his career is finished.

○ ○ ○

1950s

In 1950, Dr. Cary Middlecoff observes Hogan's miraculous return, with apparently the same swing that a pre-accident Hogan had used, with increasing success. Although Tour stats are few, it is obvious that Hogan is now consistently hitting the highest percentage of fairways and greens on Tour. He wins the U.S. Open at Merion. The secret is paying big dividends, and the public's curiosity is revitalized in the wake of Hogan's amazing comeback.

In 1951, Royal Hogan, Ben's older brother, proclaims, "I'm the only one he ever showed it [the secret] to," while Ben is helping Royal prepare for his opening match in the U.S. Amateur Championship. Whatever the secret is doesn't hold up, however, as Royal is eliminated in the first round. Hogan wins the Masters and the U.S. Open at Oakland Hills and continues to keep his trump cards tucked out of sight.

At the 1953 British Open in Carnoustie, John Derr, a CBS broadcaster covering the championship, reports that Hogan gave him "five factors critical to every golfer. . . . And yet it was never the same five things with everybody." (See chapter 5 for an explanation of the actual five factors.)

By the autumn of 1953, after Hogan wins his third major championship of the year at Carnoustie—completing the Triple Crown—the hunt for the secret turns into an international frenzy and a flurry of speculation. One news story reports it as a twenty-minute training routine that Hogan practices every morning when he wakes up, apparently still in his pajamas. (At the time, it wasn't commonly known that Hogan's first hour out of bed each day was spent in a hot Epsom salts bath to ease the pain in his aching legs.) CBS-TV is negotiating a special interview to discuss the secret, but the deal falls through.

Then, in 1954, Hogan accepts *Life* magazine's offer for exclusive rights to unveil his "mysterious secret," to be published the following year. *Life* runs a preliminary article on April 5, 1954, asking some touring pros for their thoughts on the secret behind Hogan's now legendary golf swing. Each has his own widely differing opinion, which reveals the infant state of golf swing analysis at that time. Claude Harmon observes Hogan's body not turning but sliding forward during the downswing, led by the left hip. George Fazio notes that Hogan keeps his shoulders level and thus creates a symmetrical arc similar to a baseball swing. Mike Turnesa sees Hogan opening his clubface more at address to prevent his dreaded hook.

Fred Gronaue is among the few to notice that Hogan keeps his right knee in place as a pivotal point around which his body coils and returns through the impact area in perfect balance. Sam Snead sees Hogan shortening his swing and staying behind the ball to hit higher trajectory shots.

Hogan's feisty and sometimes bitter rival, Gene Sarazen, notices Hogan's use of pronation to open the clubface wider than normal to help prevent a hook. Sarazen says that today no self-respecting professional uses pronation. He claims it is like a pill taken to cure one ill that soon requires another pill to remedy the side effects of the first one.

After beating Hogan in the 1955 U.S. Open, Jack Fleck professes that his inspired play is the result of finding the master's secret. "He might have used a secret," Hogan later tells *Life* magazine, "but it wasn't mine." (On the final hole, with Hogan poised to win a record fifth U.S. Open, the golf gods inexplicably abandon their disciple. Hogan's foot slips, and the old demon hook, rarely seen since his comeback, snaps his drive into the deep rough. Thus ends his last realistic chance to win his favorite of all championships.) Immediately following his defeat, a despondent Hogan announces his retirement from tournament golf; however, he will often return to compete in the Masters and U.S. Open over the next several years.

Hogan, now entering the twilight of his competitive years, feels free at last to have some fun with his unsolicited notoriety. Quoted in *Life* magazine, he plays his fans along with remarks like, "It [the secret] is easy to see, if I tell you where to look." He goes on about his discovery and daily practice sessions, saying, "It was like learning to play golf all over again."

On August 8, 1955, the highly anticipated *Life* feature on Hogan's secret at last hits the newsstands. Herein Hogan explains that long ago, when the Scottish pros came to America, they taught pronation, a movement that involves rolling the hands to the right on the backswing and then rolling them back to the left on the downswing. "In itself, pronation is no cure for a hook. If anything, it helps to promote one," Hogan says. "But . . . I had added two adjustments, which on paper made pronation hook-proof, without any loss of distance. The first was in the grip. I moved my left hand so that the thumb was almost directly on top of the shaft. The second adjustment, which is the real meat of the 'secret,' was nothing more than a twist or a cocking of the left wrist."

Some skeptics wonder, Is that all there is to it? How do you do that? Others believe that Hogan isn't telling the whole story and is taking *Life* and its readership for a ride. Many average golfers feel discouraged by the end of the article, where Hogan adds, "I doubt if it [the secret] will be worth a doggone to the weekend duffer and it will ruin a bad golfer."

Two years later, Hogan's *Five Lessons: The Modern Fundamentals of Golf* is published and becomes an immediate hit. Some conjecture that with this enduring best seller—which today remains a sacred text to professional and amateur alike—Hogan may be answering his critics by saying, in effect, "Here's the best shovel I can give you, now go dig out your game like I did."

o o o

1960s

In a decade of civil unrest and accelerated social change, public interest in Hogan's fundamentals and the secret gradually declines. Power players like Arnold Palmer and Jack Nicklaus, now seen by millions on television, become the new forces in professional golf.

Hogan almost realizes his dream of winning a fifth U.S. Open in 1960 at Cherry Hills. In the Saturday 36-hole final rounds, Hogan hits 27 consecutive fairways and 34 consecutive greens in regulation. Dow Finsterwald describes Hogan's performance as "the finest exhibition with irons I've ever seen." In spite of his balky flatstick (34 putts in the morning, 35 in the afternoon), he is tied for the lead when his approach to the final 17th green lands in perfect position but spins back into the water. Usually not one to look back, Hogan later admits that "there isn't a month goes by that that [loss] doesn't cut my guts out."

Hogan turns his attention to creating golf clubs instead of golf swings. The new club-making company bearing his name, now owned by American Machine and Foundry (AMF), is busy supplying a growing demand for his signature Apex forged irons and persimmon woods.

In 1965, Hogan wins a classic match against Sam Snead on *Shell's Wonderful World of Golf*, where he routinely hits every fairway and every green in regulation. During this decade, he competes in three more U.S. Opens but never again makes the top ten.

The decade also ushers in a more upright swing, perhaps best typified by a young Jack Nicklaus, in marked contrast to Hogan's flatter swing plane. Many touring pros (such as Tom Weiskopf, Tom Kite, Jerry Pate, and others) adopt the upright swing, which features the hands high on the backswing and high on the finish. Where Hogan's swing involves a level body turn with arms kept close to the torso, the upright swing follows a more up-down-up motion, with the "flying elbow" that will preoccupy golf swing analysts for the next twenty years.

"Most people are too upright because they disconnect the arms from the body," Hogan observes. He says he can't understand why people would choose to swing a golf club like that.

○ ○ ○

1970s

The Ben Hogan Company is now one of the top-selling manufacturers of golf equipment, represented in almost every pro shop in the country. As the lure of Hogan's mystique begins to fade from the public mind, mainstream golfers in this era continue to swing upright and take on the inverted C look, modeled perfectly by a young Johnny Miller, along with Hale Irwin, Weiskopf, Kite, and others. The inverted C occurs in the finish of an upright swing as the legs, back, and arms create the visual of a backward C. The force of this swing puts tremendous compression on the lower back, and in later years, many golfers will need extensive therapy and sometimes surgery to repair the damage. (It is interesting to note that Hogan, who probably hit more golf balls than any other dozen players combined, never spoke of or appeared to have any back problems.)

Searching for a way to minimize back damage and create more ball-striking consistency, many golfers in the last half of the seventies start looking back to the compact swing of the now-legendary Ben Hogan. The question of whether he had revealed all of his secret also begins to attract renewed interest in the golfing world.

In the April 1978 issue of *GOLF* magazine, Hogan's longtime friend Jimmy Demaret is quoted once again: "I think the key to Hogan's swing was the ready position—when he dropped his hands into the slot. I believe this was the real 'secret.' He always talked about it. It's a unique move that took the amount of concentration and the willingness and time to practice that only Ben Hogan brought to the game."

Meanwhile, Hogan remains silent, letting his best-selling book and a new generation of speculators do all the talking.

○ ○ ○

1980s

Hogan is still chairman of the board and involved in the day-to-day operations of his successful company. He maintains his daily ritual of practice and plays a few holes here and there. "I try to find out something new about golf every day," Hogan says. Not until halfway through this decade will the public hear more about the secret.

Mike Adams, one of the game's top golf instructors, quoted in John Andrisani's *The Hogan Way*, tells of his firsthand experience with Hogan: "In 1984, after watching Hogan hit about 100 balls at Shady Oaks, I commented that the dish angle of his left wrist increased, becoming more concave as a result of keeping the upper part of his left arm tight to his chest on the downswing." According to Adams, Hogan pauses, bends over to pick up his cigarette, then looks him right in the eyes and says, "Son, that's the secret."

In 1985, in an interview with Nick Seitz from the new foreword to *Five Lessons: The Modern Fundamentals of Golf*, Hogan casts a new light on one of his earlier revelations: "Training myself, I would roll the face open as *fast* and as *far* as I could. With this technique, I could hit the ball straight and farther."

In 1986, John Schlee publishes his book *Maximum Golf*, featuring insights and instruction that he gleaned from Hogan during their years together in the late sixties and early seventies.

In a 1989 interview with *Golf Digest*, Hogan is asked why many pros who tried his secret were unsuccessful in eliminating their problem hooks. His reply: "I'll only say they weren't doing it correctly."

○ ○ ○

1990s

The Ben Hogan Company becomes a subsidiary of its new Japanese parent, Cosmo World, with Hogan now little more than a figurehead.

In June 1991, *Golf Digest* is approached by Dave Hueber, then president of the Ben Hogan Company. Hueber says that Hogan is now willing to "unlock the vault" and give the world a *new* secret that can shave ten strokes off the average amateur's score and enable touring pros to shoot in the 50s. Hogan suggests that the new secret is simple enough to be learned in a single lesson. Has Hogan really unearthed another gem? Or did he disclose only part of his secret back in 1955 and now is finally willing to tell all? Or is he hoping to take his mystery tour out for one last lucrative round? The deal never happens because *Golf Digest* decides not to pony up the six-figure fee that Hogan demands.

In March 1994, *Golf Digest* runs a story by Guy Yocom, proclaiming that he and Hank Haney have finally determined Hogan's "real secret." The gist is that Hogan cocks his left wrist on the backswing (previously noted in the 1955 *Life* article) and then bows the left wrist through the impact area (previously noted in Hogan's *Five Lessons*), a technique that keeps the clubhead moving down the target line longer. Tiger Woods later develops a similar move for his famed "stinger" 2-iron shot. The article also contains the views of some top players, many of whom feel that Hogan still hasn't told the whole story. From the *Golf Digest* article, here are some of their observations:

Ken Venturi: "Hogan told me what his real secret was under the condition that I not tell anybody else. So I won't say what it is other than to tell you that his secret was up here" (points to his head).

Dean Reinmuth: Thinks Hogan curbed the amount of clubface rotation by keeping his shaft angle at impact consistent with the shaft angle at address.

Chuck Cook: Hogan found stiffer shafts that didn't allow his clubface to close, thereby allowing him to fade the ball consistently.

Jack Burke Jr.: "Ben used his right hand to control the clubface better than anyone, ever. He found a way to set the club at the top of the backswing the same way every time."

Dr. Cary Middlecoff: "Ben pushed his right elbow right in front of his stomach on the downswing . . . so far forward that it was almost impossible for the clubface to close and hook the ball."

Gardner Dickinson: Hogan moved the ball forward and his hands back behind the ball at address to promote his power fade.

Bob Toski: "He stabilized the force of the blow with his left arm and hand, keeping his left arm moving [on line] well past impact."

Johnny Miller: "To me, Hogan was a little bit like Jesus in that he talked in parables. He gave you the picture, but he really didn't give the whole picture."

The March 1994 *Golf Digest* issue also includes an analysis by Hank Haney (with Guy Yocom) on the keys to the "real secret" and how to apply it to your game. Haney believes, as many people still do today, that Hogan's secret is not for every-one. Haney demonstrates three aspects of the secret—a weak left-hand grip, the rotation of the left hand and forearm on the takeaway, and a cupped left wrist. He also shows how to manip-ulate the club on the backswing and adjust the left shoulder on the downswing to keep it on plane. The gist is that Hogan's swing secrets mainly address the tendency to hook, not a com-mon problem for the average golfer, and require special attention to timing.

In July 1997, Hogan passes away, and the golfing public will lose its final chance to hear the master's own revelations on this controversial, elusive, evolving mystery called "the secret."

○ ○ ○

2000

By the turn of the century, many feel that Hogan has carried an entirely new secret with him to his final resting place. Some con-tinue to believe that he'd been parceling out his hard-earned nuggets a mere crumb at a time and only when he could turn a dollar. But even his most envious critics have to admit that Hogan's game amply validated its strong market value and that he'd been almost as good a businessman as he was a golfer.

In Andrisani's *The Hogan Way*, Mike McGetrick, a top PGA teaching professional, is quoted as saying that Hogan's secret is more involved than one single swing thought. "His keys include moving the left hand more to the left, fanning the clubface open in the takeaway to create a flatter swing plane . . . and delaying the release of the club."

In 2004, in Jody Vasquez's *Afternoons with Mr. Hogan*, he states that Hogan gave *him* the secret, which he describes as a turning of the right knee inward when addressing the ball. The idea is to maintain a firm right knee throughout the backswing. More than thirty years earlier, Hogan had given a more thorough explanation of this concept to John Schlee. John used it to develop the "impact address position," which he describes in his *Maximum Golf* book and video.

○ ○ ○

Sam Snead was quoted as saying, "Anybody can say he's got a secret if he won't tell what it is." Sometimes even when you reveal a secret, as Hogan did, people don't believe you, and they insist it must be something else.

It appears that Hogan actually had two major secrets. One was the parent, the other its child. The first he gave to the public again and again. Paradoxically, it remained hidden from most people—by their choice, not Hogan's. The second secret, or set of secrets, he kept under wraps, later parceling out fragments over the years but never giving the complete picture during his lifetime.

From my lifetime of studying, practicing, and playing the fundamentals of Hogan's discoveries, this is how I see it:

1. The first is the secret of Hogan's *success*. This one resided in his heart, the engine that drove and sustained him through endless hours of digging and competition. If you work hard and long enough, he said many times, you can't help but achieve some degree of success. It's not a secret that real satisfaction and fulfillment come from sticking with your own dream through thick and thin. That's all I'm doing, he said in so many words. Now why don't you try it for yourselves?

Typically, almost everyone wanted a more alchemical revelation, a secret elixir they could swallow and awaken the next morning with a lower handicap. They heard Hogan's words but denied his message.

2. The second is the secret of Hogan's *technology*. This one was gradually unveiled throughout the decades, as noted previously in the chronology. Some of it Hogan revealed in *Life* magazine and later in his book *Five Lessons: The Modern Fundamentals of Golf*. The rest came in pieces—given in confidence to individuals like John Schlee, Ken Venturi, and very few others—and culminated in the "missing link" ingredient that completes the recipe for Hogan's mechanical marvel.

Hogan's secret techniques are the natural offspring of his first and most vital wisdom: the highest priority must be a commitment to the work and discipline of self-realization, the "secret" fountain from which one's own magic may spring forth.

○ ○ ○

For most of us, golf is a part-time sport. For Hogan, of course, it was his whole life. Yet without devoting every waking hour to the game as he did, we can still take advantage of what he achieved and left behind for us. Just as he advised John Schlee, we can use his treasure of knowledge not to mimic, but to learn as a starting point to help us build our own better game.

In that spirit, I offer the following instruction as another way, in Hogan's words, "to find out something new about golf every day."

The Technology of Hogan's Secret

As mentioned earlier, Hogan discussed "five factors critical to every golfer" with the CBS broadcaster John Derr at the 1953 British Open in Carnoustie. Derr later observed, "Yet it was never the same five things with everybody." This makes sense if you consider that Hogan adapted variations of his fundamentals to fit the recipient's game at the time. He was aware that too much too soon might only confuse and frustrate. To those few people who gained audience to his insights, he was a thoughtful, considerate counselor who understood that every golfer's goals, abilities, and needs are unique.

At the same time, Hogan also realized—through years of intense study and practice—that some key fundamentals are essential to develop a repeatable, effective golf swing. To win professional tournaments (or to perform well in your own golf matches), you must learn and practice specific coordinated movements to create accurate golf shots, day in and day out.

The "five factors" highlight important swing movements and are essential to learning the fundamentals of the Hogan golf swing. (Some are included in Hogan's books, and others are not.) I have incorporated these factors into the Legendary Golf System, which includes Hogan's swing secrets and insights, in a simple instructional plan that virtually anyone can adopt in a short time and enjoy for a lifetime.

○ ○ ○

Many golfers have asked, "If Hogan's secret was mostly about curing his hook, what good will it do me if I usually slice the ball?" In his 1955 *Life* magazine revelation, Hogan had this to say about slicing: "The better swing you have and the better player you become—as far as hitting the ball, that is—the more definitely you become a hooker." In other words, you can best resolve the slicing tendency by creating a sound swing, not by patching some solution over a particular problem. Once you have trained yourself in the correct swing movements and use the proper grip, you will tend to draw the ball or hit it straighter. And because Hogan's technique eliminated a severe hook from his swing, it will have little cause to appear in yours, either.

When Hogan discovered the swing techniques that comprised his secret, he didn't believe that it would benefit all golfers. Beginning in 1969, however, John Schlee found that by learning and practicing Hogan's simple but crucial movements, almost any average golfer can find immediate improvement in ball striking and control. Schlee confirmed this time and again by successfully teaching Hogan's fundamentals to thousands of students at his Maximum Golf Schools during the 1980s.

○ ○ ○

As you will see, Ben Hogan's secret involves the *learned* ability to use a turning body to propel the arms and the hands through the hitting area in a precise and consistent manner. The key in this statement is "a *learned* ability."

The only way to learn to do something correctly is to have the proper information, coupled with an effective plan. I have outlined the proper information in the instructional plan that follows. In plain, straightforward steps, I'll show you how to use it effectively.

Hogan explained to John that each component involved in the secret has its own duties that first must be understood by the golfer. Second, the components must be used *in conjunction with one another* for the swing to work successfully.

In this section, I explain *what* the five essential factors are and *why* they are necessary for a successful golf swing. Then, in the following instructional chapter, I will demonstrate *how* to use them.

The five factors relate to right knee, left hip, arms, hands, and left elbow. The first two factors are lower-body movements that set up a strong coil on the backswing and then trigger the release of the coil during the downswing.

① THE RIGHT KNEE

WHAT: In the address position, the right knee is set inward and held in place to limit the rotation of the right hip, thereby creating the body coil in the backswing.

WHY: Clubhead speed is determined by coil tension and release of that tension through the hitting area. No coil, no speed.

In the case of Jody Vasquez, the author of *Afternoons with Mr. Hogan*, the angle of the right knee was the most important key for Jody to grasp at the time. Hogan called this move "the secret" so Jody could work on mastering it without complicating that particular lesson with other untimely details. The angle of the right knee is definitely a component of the secret—but only one part of it that Hogan had taught John Schlee thirty years earlier.

The right knee set inward at address.

The right knee remains set at top of the swing.

② THE LEFT HIP

WHAT: The downswing is initiated by rotating the left hip as fast as possible with minimal lateral motion. The arms and hands *follow* as they release into the hitting area. Chronic slicers invariably do the reverse: they start the downswing with the hands and arms, which tends to yank the lower body rearward into a reverse pivot, causing the clubhead to cut across the ball and thus create a slice or a pulled shot.

WHY: Starting the downswing by turning the knees and left hip initiates Hogan's famous chain action, which keeps the body's movements unfolding in sequence. The left hip is the last part to coil in the backswing and the first part to uncoil in the downswing. Imagine your legs and hips as the handle of a whip and the clubhead as its tip. You crack the whip by moving the handle first, while the chain action multiplies and creates tremendous speed as it races out to the tip (clubhead).

Tom Lehman and Jose Maria Olazabal are excellent examples of a fast, powerful hip turn that initiates their downswing.

○ ○ ○

The left hip initiates the downswing.

The next three components work closely together to transfer the energy of the hip turn to the clubhead for optimum distance and direction control. These factors help ensure that your clubface squares up to the target line without conscious hand manipulation or interference.

③ THE ARMS

WHAT: The arms have the critical task of bringing the hands into the impact zone precisely every time. They must work together, and the only way they can work together is to actively set them up with the *elbows turned inward toward each other*.

This unites the arms so they can move together as one coordinated unit. Hogan explained to John Schlee that the arms need to function as "one big arm." Betsy King, a consistent winner on the LPGA Tour, is an excellent example of keeping arms and the elbows together at address and throughout the swing. Vijay Singh practices this move by keeping a cloth tucked under his left arm *throughout his entire swing*.

The elbows set inward at address.

WHY: If you do not assign the arms the specific job of working as a unit, they tend to work independently and inconsistently.

In *Five Lessons: The Modern Fundamentals of Golf*, Hogan constantly emphasizes that both forearms and the wrists should be kept together as long as possible throughout the swing.

Hogan emphasized to John that the arms must be activated in the setup: "Bring them as close together as you can without creating tension—but create activation." He went on to say that keeping the arms positioned close together on the backswing also creates a proper, consistent swing plane because the arms dictate the plane of the swing.

Because the arms dictate the swing plane, the left arm should move directly across the chest and the right shoulder during the takeaway—not above or below—while the right arm and elbow naturally fold into the torso. Keeping the elbows turned inward, coupled with proper body rotation, creates the right swing plane automatically.

Notice how this move works for players like Vijay Singh, Jay Haas, Kenny Perry, Justin Leonard, and many others.

The left arm slides straight across the chest.

④ THE HANDS

Make the hands part of a controlled plan, rather than leaving them free to seek their own part in the swing. The hands not only grip the club, but they must learn their role in the coiling and uncoiling movement that creates a powerful release of the clubhead through the ball.

Hogan explains in detail how to establish his version of the Vardon grip in his *Five Lessons*. Our concern here is with how to use this grip for power and accuracy.

○ ○ ○

WHAT: The grip is your only physical connection to the golf club, and it must be set up correctly. The grip determines how the rest of your body is able to perform throughout the swing. An improper grip can restrict the hands and adversely affect the movements of the arms, shoulders, hips, and legs during the swing.

When you actively roll the left hand and forearm to the right (pronate) in the backswing, you are coiling extra energy into the hands. Coil them on the backswing, and let them release as they uncoil through the hitting area. Keep a soft grip with limber hands and forearms; otherwise, they cannot perform this important task.

(During the first half of the 1900s, pronation was considered a "handsy" move to help control the clubhead, especially with hickory shafts. Hogan was an advocate of pronation and supination [turning upward, the opposite of pronation] in the modern golf swing. He told John Schlee to forget about this terminology

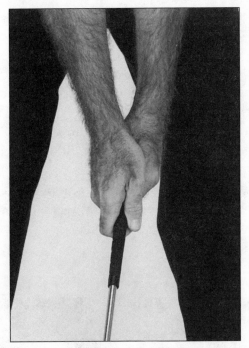

Hogan's modified (weak) Vardon grip.

and focus on the movement itself: roll the hands to the right to initiate the backswing, then let them roll to the left on the downswing.)

WHY: When Hogan described certain components of the secret in his famous 1955 *Life* magazine revelation, he explained how he changed his grip to a weak position by placing the thumb of his left hand on top of the shaft. The weak grip enabled Hogan to add his little twist to create a greater coil and a longer delay in the release of the club. He had found that a strong grip restricts these essential movements.

With these two changes, he created his hook-proof swing, which also added significant clubhead speed as his hands uncoiled.

In a new foreword to *Five Lessons* with Nick Seitz (1985 edition), Hogan stated, "I rolled the face of the club *open* and *away* from the ball . . . and the *faster* I could *rotate* it, the more distance I got." This key is one reason a 5-foot-7, 135-pound man could hit his persimmon driver 300-plus yards when he wanted to.

With the hands in Hogan's weak grip position, they have an opportunity to move in three different ways: up and down, back and forth, or turning from side to side.

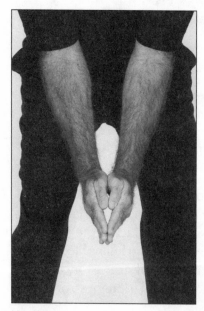

Hands up.

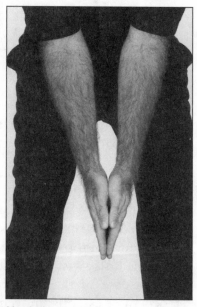

Hands down.

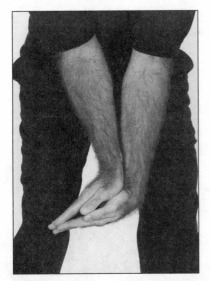

Hands back.

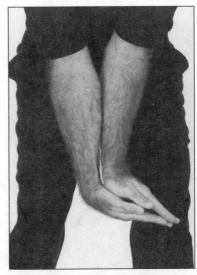

Hands forth.

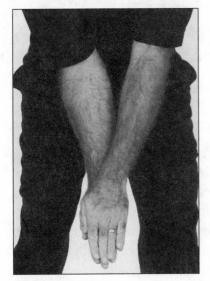

Hands side right.

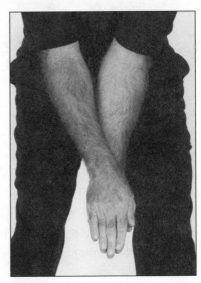

Hands side left.

The standard clubhead position at takeaway.

The takeaway position with Hogan's "little twist."

These three types of hand movements work together in forming the left wristcock and the coiling of the hands. Notice in the photo on the left how the angle of the clubhead is in the traditional straight up or perpendicular position recommended by most modern-day teachers. The open clubhead position (see the photo on the right) is a result of rolling the hands with the extra "little twist."

⑤ THE LEFT ELBOW

Even though Hogan never mentioned it in his books, he told John that this final factor is vitally important: the responsibility of the *left elbow*. Because it has escaped notice in the golfing world all these years, I call it the "missing link" in the ongoing analysis of Hogan's secret. (I devote a special section to this in the following instruction.)

WHAT: It is imperative that the left elbow rotate toward the left hip on the downswing.

By keeping both elbows close together, the left elbow will naturally want to turn in toward the left hip, but it must be trained to ensure that it performs this vital function every time. This movement squares up the clubface as it comes into the ball.

WHY: If the left elbow isn't assigned the important task of turning toward the left hip, it tends to wander outward and move the clubhead off course. This usually results in an open clubface and a slice. The left elbow move also eliminates the feeling that you need to consciously manipulate the club (that is, get handsy) to bring it in square to the target.

The left elbow—key to squaring the clubface.

6

The Legendary
Golf System

After back injuries forced John Schlee to leave the PGA Tour in 1978, he devoted himself full time to teaching. He immediately began to develop a new and unusual instruction program by transforming his lessons from Ben Hogan into a system he called Maximum Golf. His program included some of the essential points discussed in the previous chapter, along with other basic training techniques and concepts that he'd learned during his years with Hogan.

Here, to complete the final instructional package that includes the fundamentals of Hogan's swing secrets and key points from Maximum Golf, I have combined the essentials into what I call the Legendary Golf System. I consider it a complete and final summation of all the key elements of Hogan's golf swing, arranged in a simple format that the average golfer can understand, use, and enjoy.

This training program takes a bit of practice to work effectively, but it's not so daunting when you realize that in a matter of weeks, you can learn and apply to your game the secrets that took Hogan at least forty years of steady digging to discover. As I began to comprehend and apply the depth of Hogan's hard-won wisdom to my own game, I felt as if someone had handed me a big bag of gold nuggets and said, "Here's all you need to buy your ticket to golfer's heaven."

I've worked hard to make the Legendary Golf System simple and easy to learn. It is based on a unique and highly effective method of practicing Hogan's fundamentals by using slow swing motions.

Why Slow Swing Motions?

How can your body perform movements in a golf swing going full speed when you haven't mastered them in slow motion? The simple truth is, it can't.

You learn to walk before you can run; you learn your ABCs before you can read. Likewise, to own a sound golf swing that operates reliably at full power, you learn precise swing motions by going through them slowly until they become natural and comfortable. Most important, you condition your mind and muscles to execute these moves *without consciously thinking*.

Martial artists know that it's essential to train themselves using precise, deliberate movements on a regular basis. With consistent training, their practiced moves flow automatically in the heat of battle where there is no time to think, only to act and react at flash speed.

Learning your swing at a slower pace enables you to watch it take shape and *feel* the flow of energy as you move through each position. This will prove far easier and more effective than trying to adjust movements *during* your normal golf swing when you're moving fast and a dozen thoughts are jumping through your mind.

Or take Harvey Penick's word for it. In his classic *Little Red Book*, he said, "A slow motion swing develops the golf muscles, implants the correct club positions in your golfing brain—and doesn't smash the chandelier." This is what we're looking for in developing a legendary golf swing.

As an effective practice tool for slow-motion swing training, I recommend a shortened golf club about 24 inches in length. The club should have a real golf grip and a real clubhead for weighting purposes. This short club may not be essential, but it will greatly facilitate your training sessions because you will be using a proper golf grip. You can get an old club cut to size and regripped or, if you need help in getting one, contact me and I'll be happy to hook you up.

For optimum results, these motions should be practiced every day. Studies have shown that any habit—in this case, the correct movements that create a solid, repeatable golf swing—can be learned in less than thirty days if practiced regularly. In sixty days, with regular practice and play, they are close to becoming second nature.

The Mind Is the Coach

In his *Maximum Golf* video, John summed up his approach this way: "The mind is the coach, and the body is the team. You can't fire the coach and you can't trade the team. You need to educate the coach so he can lead the team."

At this point, I invite you to assume the role of head coach and look at the various parts of your body as lifetime members of your team. The pay may not be that great, but the results can be priceless.

For now, let's imagine that you've signed up for a coaching seminar on the Legendary Golf System. I'll assume the role of seminar host and temporary head trainer. My task is to introduce you to our Hogan-based swing system, its training concepts and coaching tools. When you complete the seminar, I hope you will return to your own "schools" to train and coach your team players to higher levels of accomplishment and satisfaction.

Most of all, I hope you will enjoy feeling some of Ben Hogan's magic in your game. It's a gift you can't buy, but you can learn and enjoy it as much as you desire.

First, we'll meet the team players and review their duties in the setup. Second, we'll study the motions involved for coaching our players through the backswing, the downswing, and the follow-through. We will identify, explain, and slowly repeat each movement to help you demonstrate for yourself the fundamentals of Hogan's golf swing as you proceed to make them your own. In doing so, we will enter Hogan's inner circle, a realm previously known only by his few select devotees.

If you haven't read Hogan's *Five Lessons: The Modern Fundamentals of Golf*, I heartily recommend doing so. It is excellent foundation material to help you incorporate the following instructions. However, it isn't my purpose here simply to rehash the material in Hogan's book. We will review his main points and his later revelations, along with new material I've included (such as the "missing link" and other details). They are all synchronized into one program in the Legendary Golf System.

THE SET-UP: GETTING THE RIGHT START

Using a sound, consistent setup is the first step in creating a repeatable swing.

I am amazed at the lack of importance people give to the setup. Too many beginners don't even think of it. Their setup is different almost every time, which leads to a variety of results when they swing at the ball.

In a world of infinite possibilities, we're looking for some reliable constants in our golf game. A good setup routine is one of them.

Many players also believe they must feel comfortable when addressing the ball, when in reality, the setup is one of the most awkward still positions in sports today.

Remember Hogan's famous note that if you do everything just the opposite of what your body wants to do, you may be able to fashion a good golf swing? No matter how odd it may feel at first, a proper setup will soon feel natural with sufficient practice.

The setup is supposed to line you up with *where you want to go* from where you are. The ball is your ammunition, but your target is the goal, your utmost priority. With that in mind, following are the three steps to a good setup.

First, align your mind to a specific target *before* you address the ball. Locking in a target lets your body know exactly what you want it to do. I suggest reading Printer Bowler's book *The Cosmic Laws of Golf (and everything else)* to develop your target-locking powers. His "Magic Triangle" technique is simple, fun, and amazingly effective.

Setup, front view.

Setup, side view.

Second, align your body to your chosen target. Hogan always reminded John to get in the habit of lining up to a specific object. You can practice using any object as a target at home or on the practice range.

Third, develop your own procedure to set up to a target and assume a consistent address position over the ball. This is your setup routine. Adjust it as necessary over time, but use the same movements and time frame when you address every shot.

John Schlee clocked a number of Tour players in the late sixties and found that the ones who played well never varied their routines (from selecting a club to the finish of their swing) by more than a second.

Create your own setup routine that aligns you to your target—and stick with it. A regular setup also provides an important sense of continuity for your game. It can help you feel at home, especially when your mind and body find themselves in unfamiliar territory.

Here are key checkpoints for your team players in the classic Hogan setup:

1. The right foot is set perpendicular to the target line to restrict the right hip and create coil power on the backswing. The left foot is slightly open to the target line to allow the lower body more freedom to release through the hitting area.

    During the setup, we are looking for a balanced, solid foundation as you position your feet on the ground.

    Set your weight between the ball and the instep of each foot—away from the toes, away from the heels. Distribute the weight evenly between the right foot and the left foot. This creates a balanced foundation.

    I have my students set their feet shoulder-width apart for the 5-iron and adjust accordingly. Move increasingly wider with each club up to the driver and narrower down to the wedges. Keep the width of your stance within the boundaries that allow you to make your full turn and stay balanced.

Setup, feet.

2. Activate the legs by flexing the knees level to the ground.

The legs, our biggest source of power in the swing, must be *activated* to generate this power. Flexing your knees until the weight is centered in the middle of your feet will achieve proper activation. Turn your right knee slightly inward to create a feeling of pressure on the inside of the right foot.

Athletes from all sports—such as basketball, football, hockey, and tennis—prepare their bodies with this flexed-knee, ready position. Be sure that both knees are flexed evenly so they remain level to the ground.

John made it easy for me to picture this. He said, "Pretend you are the shortstop for the New York Yankees and you are getting into a ready position, just before the pitch."

Setup, legs, front view.

Setup, legs, side view.

3. The hips are level and slightly open to the target line.

Hogan felt that the hips were a vital part of the setup, in addition to their movement in the swing. When you set your feet and activate your legs, be sure the hips are level to the ground and slightly open to the target line. (Your right knee turned inward promotes the slightly open hips.) When your body spins and turns through the hitting area, the open hips enable the left side to clear out of the way so that your momentum toward the target is uninhibited.

Setup, hips.

4. The hands grip the club with the left thumb on top of the shaft and the palms facing each other. (Hogan illustrates this grip in detail in his book *Five Lessons*.)

Hogan explained to John that the Vardon overlap grip was the better grip to use because you have more fingers on the club than in the interlocking grip (used by Jack Nicklaus and Tiger Woods). You also create the unity of both hands, which you don't get with the ten-finger grip. If you feel that your hands are too small to hold the club more in the fingers, John always said, "Get smaller grips."

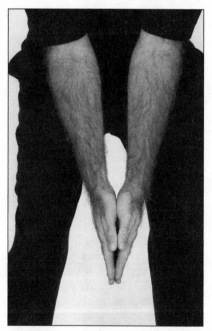

Setup, palms facing each other.

Setup, Hogan's weak grip.

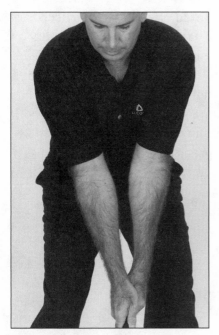

Setup, arms, front view.

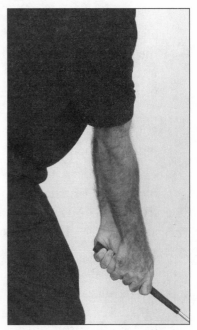

Setup, arms, back view.

5. The arms are extended down, and the right tricep is gently resting against the upper torso.

   When you assume the setup position with your arms, let them hang naturally toward the ground as much as possible as you grip the club. Activate the forearms by turning the elbows toward each other until a three-inch gap (more or less) remains between them. This movement will cause the inner sides of your forearms to rotate slightly upward as the elbows move closer together. Keep the forearms and hands relaxed as you activate them.

Once the arms are activated, let the right tricep rest against your torso. As Hogan said, "It helps, you will find, if the upper part of the right arm adheres as closely as possible to the side of the chest." This will keep the right elbow in its most effective position throughout the swing.

The arms are your connection to the turning body. If you don't activate your arms in the setup, they will tend to work independently and unpredictably during the swing.

6. The shoulders are responsible for the transfer of energy from the body to the arms and hands. They must be kept soft and relaxed to do their job properly.

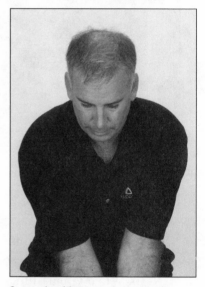

In the setup, the shoulders have one purpose, and that is to be relaxed. Energy cannot flow freely through tensed muscles.

When you view your setup in the mirror, be sure there is some slope to your shoulders. If you don't see any slope, you are probably holding tension in the shoulders. Practice relaxing your shoulders, and let them descend away from your ears.

Setup, shoulders.

7. Your torso—your back, chest, and midsection—must be erect and activated.

In the setup, Hogan said that activating the stomach and lower-back muscles will create a feeling of unity

Setup, torso, front view.

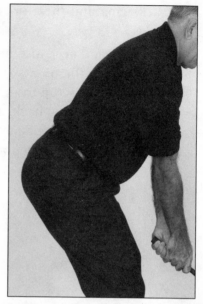

Setup, torso, back view.

between the upper body and lower body. The angle of the spine must be straight, not bowed over. This setup will give you a solid, integrated feeling that your whole body is part of one continuous movement throughout the swing.

The midsection muscles must be activated, or turned on, to create a stimulating sensation. The feeling is similar to knowing that you're about to get a friendly poke in the stomach. Activated, but not rigid.

The lower-back muscles are automatically activated when you keep your back straight and you bend slightly from the hips.

If you fail to unify the lower body with the upper body, it's nearly impossible to create a strong coil during the backswing and therefore a powerful release on the down-swing.

8. The head and neck also must remain erect and on a straight line with the torso.

View your setup from the side to check for proper alignment of your head, back, and legs. You should see a straight line from your tailbone to the top of your head.

The eyes should be looking straight ahead as they view

the ball. If the head bends forward, the chin will be in the way of the turning shoulders, and your eyes need to look upward to see the ball. If the head bends backward, you must look downward to see the ball. Either way has an adverse effect on the rest of your alignment and swing performance. Your eyes naturally want to view objects straight on, and your body will want to adjust itself to accommodate the eyes. Before—not during—the swing is the time to make these adjust-ments.

The head, neck, and back are aligned.

During his years of experimentation, Hogan found that a repeatable golf swing must be based on a repeatable setup procedure, much like the eight steps we have reviewed in this chapter. The idea of a consistent setup was not common knowledge in Hogan's early days, and it had to be unearthed and refined along with many other golf techniques we now take for granted.

Hogan also found it essential to keep the entire body in a state of *relaxed activation* during the setup and throughout the entire swing. The feeling you want in a proper setup is as follows: muscles are soft and limber, yet alert and ready to flow. You must keep them soft—especially the hands, arms, and shoulders—so they are free to conduct energy with smooth power and speed as you move through the golf swing.

So start creating more consistency in your game by following a regular steup procedure. Use our eight steps to create a personal checklist you will use *for each and every swing* you make. In other words, make your setup routine an integral part of your golf swing.

Practice at home until you are able to assume an activated, relaxed setup in fifteen to twenty-five seconds. That's an average time for most Tour players when they address the ball, get set, and swing away.

With a solid setup in place, we're now ready to train our team players in the use of Hogan's legendary swing movements.

THE SWING: START TO FINISH

When you turn your shoulders and keep your arms close together on the backswing, you will find your natural swing plane.

—Hogan's instruction to John Schlee

Backswing Phase I—The First Move

Begin by cocking the wrists and rolling open the clubface, as the shoulders turn, until the butt of the club passes the middle of the right knee.

Hogan discovered three significant actions crucial to developing a good backswing: the wristcock, rolling the clubface open to coil the hands, and the shoulder turn.

Backswing phase I—the first move.

These key actions are performed at the same time during the golf swing. It may be helpful to practice only the wristcock and coiling the hands to isolate and develop each movement. When you are confident, execute them with the shoulder turn.

It is important to understand that the shoulder turn is just that—the turning of the shoulders as one unit. When you maintain inward pressure of the forearms, the shoulders work together. If you do not, the shoulders can and will work independently.

While you execute Phase 1, the shoulders turning will produce a feeling of rotation around the head, which should remain steady, with very little or no lateral movement to the right. Keep shoulders, arms, and hands soft and limber—no tension, no straining.

Remember, the only moving parts in Phase 1 are the shoulders turning, the wrists starting to cock, and the hands coiling. The lower body hasn't moved because the shoulders haven't turned enough to initiate any action.

Phase 1 isolates the shoulders, arms, and wrists so you can become more aware of their individual movements. Examine yourself in a mirror and look for these important checkpoints.

Checkpoints for Phase I

1. Wrists are beginning to cock.
2. Butt of the club points just above the inside of the right knee.
3. Elbows remain turned inward toward the midsection.
4. Tricep of the right arm moves slightly across the torso.
5. Right shoulder appears slightly higher than the left.

I am an advocate of that kind of teaching which stresses the exact nature and feel of movements a player makes to achieve the results he wants . . . actions that cause the result.

—*Hogan,* Five Lessons

Backswing Phase 2—Loading Up

Continue rotating the left hand and forearm clockwise and turning the shoulders until the hands have reached hip level on the backswing.

Picking up where we left off from Phase 1, we continue the shoulder rotation and the wrist-coiling motion. These *actions* cause the following *reactions*:

Backswing phase 2—loading up.

The right elbow reacts by starting to fold into the torso and point toward the ground. Notice how this motion of the folding right elbow puts your practice club on a perfect plane. This happens because *the arms dictate the plane of the swing.* Chad Campbell, a rising star on the PGA Tour, is a great example of allowing the right elbow to fold and point toward the ground, establishing his proper swing plane.

The hips react by turning slightly to the right. The left knee reacts by moving slightly toward the ball.

The hip and the left knee reaction causes some weight to move *against the inside* of the right foot. Why the inside? This is where your power buildup begins. Pressure against the inside right foot helps to keep the lower body firmly in place so it can resist the turning upper body. Hogan referred to this resistance as "retaining the angle of the right leg." (See Hogan's *Five Lessons.*)

By moving your weight *against the inside* of your right foot, you restrict the movement of the right knee, the right knee restricts the movement of the right hip, and the right hip restricts the movement of the shoulders—thereby creating what we know as backswing coil.

Checkpoints for Phase 2

1. Head remains still.
2. Shoulder turn increases.
3. Right elbow points toward the ground.
4. Upper portion of the right tricep remains against the torso.
5. Hips and left knee are turned *slightly* to the right.
6. Pressure builds on the inside of the right foot.

A full swing is nothing more or less than an extension of the short swing.

—*Hogan,* Five Lessons

Backswing Phase 3—Reaching the Top

Continue the shoulder turn until you have reached the top of your backswing without forfeiting any resistance.

Finish your coil, plain and simple.

Remember, the full shoulder turn is your ability to turn the upper body as much as you can, on the backswing, without losing resistance against the lower body. The shoulder turn is very important for storing power; a limited turn stores limited power.

Backswing phase 3—reaching the top.

The idea is to wind up your upper body in the backswing, but only as far as your shoulders can turn without swaying or bending the left arm.

Many people have been taught to turn until their clubs are parallel to the ground at the top of their backswing—regardless of each person's flexibility. Everyone is built differently. When you try to achieve this textbook position, two things often happen: (1) The arms break down by separating and bending at the left elbow, or (2) the weight rolls over to the outside of the right foot. Either way, coil resistance is weakened, resulting in less power stored for release in the downswing.

Check out Dana Quigley, the Senior Tour's "Iron Man," for a full shoulder turn while his club is far short of parallel at the top of his swing.

The action of the shoulder turn creates a wind-up for power, but a controlled wind-up without the possibility for breakdown. Your body may feel tight the first couple of times you practice Phase 3, but if you don't feel any stretching, chances are you're breaking down your arms or sliding laterally.

Checkpoints for Phase 3

1. Head remains still.
2. Shoulders turn as far as *your* limit allows.
3. Arms are still close together, with the right elbow pointing toward the ground.
4. Hip turn increases slightly but still resists the upper-body turn.
5. Left knee points toward the ball.
6. Right knee remains flexed and firmly in place.
7. Pressure continues against inside of the right foot.

> If the average golfer will only start his downswing with his hips, what a world of difference this will make in his swing and his shots, not to mention his score.
>
> —*Hogan*, Five Lessons

Downswing Phase I—The Trigger

Trigger the downswing with the left knee and left hip rotating toward the target.

The initial action of the downswing is the movement of the lower body.

It is crucial that you feel the turning sensation in your lower body as you start your downswing. This turning lower body triggers the release of energy coiled in your backswing.

Downswing phase I—the trigger.

Tiger Woods is probably the best example of a PGA Tour player who uses his hips as Hogan suggests. Tiger has said many times that he unwinds his hips "as fast as they can possibly go."

Once the motion of the lower body has activated the downswing, allow the right elbow to dive in front of the right hip. As Hogan said, "The arms don't propel this motion themselves. They are carried down by the movement of the hips." This lowering motion of the arms starts the uncoiling process of the hands. Arms and hands must remain limber to perform properly.

Where you had a cup in the back of your left wrist at the top of the backswing, you now have lost that cup. Your supple left wrist straightens out and lines up with the back of your left hand.

Checkpoints for Phase I

1. Knees and hips rotate as weight transfers to the left foot.
2. Inside of the right foot is relieved of pressure.
3. Right heel starts rising off the ground.
4. Knees, hips, and shoulders are level to the ground.
5. Arms continue to be close together.
6. Right elbow drops in front of the right hip.
7. Club shaft is perpendicular to the back.

The left leg breaks resiliently to the left, and the bulk of the weight rides forward to the left side of the left foot, the leg bows out toward the target.

—*Hogan,* Five Lessons

Downswing Phase 2— The All-Important Turn

Continue the hip turn until the hands have returned to the ball and the clubshaft is no less than parallel to the ground.

The only important feeling you should have at this point is hips-to-shoulders turning, turning, and more turning. I cannot

Downswing phase 2—the all-important turn.

emphasize enough the turning sensation you should undergo. Your spine is the center post, and you are spinning around it like a door on its hinges.

This phase of the downswing is the easiest to accomplish because we are isolating the turning muscles in the hips and the shoulders. From the end of Phase 1 to the end of Phase 2, the only significant movement in the upper body is the turning torso and shoulders. Your arms and hands are relaxed and still hanging back, waiting for their ride to the impact zone.

Remember to make a *level* turn. The left knee dictates where the left hip goes, and the right knee dictates where the right hip goes. If your knees are moving level left, then your hips will move level left, and the swing will remain on plane.

Checkpoints for Phase 2

1. Weight is toward the outside of the left foot.
2. Right heel is completely off the ground.
3. Arms remain as close together as possible.
4. Right elbow is positioned in front of the right hip.
5. Wrists remain in a cocked position.
6. Back of the left hand is perpendicular to the ground.

Familiarize yourself with these checkpoints. When you practice the motion of Phase 2, combine it with the motion of Phase 1. Remember, they are motions first and positions second. At this point, I ask you to return to the top of your backswing and go through the motion of Phase 1 of the downswing, then move into Phase 2 of the downswing, and stop right there. Make sure that all of your vital checkpoints are in place before you start the motion of Phase 3.

Before we get to Downswing Phase 3, we need to investigate an essential part of the swing—squaring the clubface—that many believe "just happens." Of course, somehow it happens, but you will have better success if you learn *how* to create the proper movement to ensure that this occurs.

This is where the "missing link" in Hogan's secret comes into play.

The Missing Link to Hogan's Secret

In *Five Lessons*, Hogan explains the idea of the left wrist uncoiling (letting it turn counterclockwise) on the downswing: the palm of the left hand faces down at the top, then faces up as it returns through the impact zone. Because of this uncoiling, the left wrist is leading through the impact zone and remains the leader through to the finish.

What Hogan doesn't fully explain is *how* this happens or *how* to develop it for your own swing. That is what I will do now.

Remember, the center post of the swing is the torso. To generate speed, the torso must turn or spin. So we coil against a resisting right side on the backswing, and we release this tension as we uncoil on the downswing.

Our players (body parts) have specific functions that they must perform during the uncoiling for the clubface to return square to the ball. How can we make sure this happens?

First, let's look at what has been generally agreed on by Hogan swing analysts:

The job of the hips and the legs? Initiate the downswing.

The job of the shoulders? Follow the turning hips.

The job of the arms? Connect the hands to the shoulders and the spinning torso.

The job of the hands? Uncoil on the downswing as they follow the arms.

Then whose job is it to consistently square up the clubface? Is it the hands'? No. Hogan repeatedly said that the hands are not to get involved in squaring up the clubface.

We're missing something here. If the spinning body brings the hands through the hitting area with speed and precision, what's the connection?

The arms.

If the arms connect the body to the hands and allow an uninterrupted flow of energy, what dictates the position of the hands in the impact zone?

The left elbow.

If the left arm remains extended and maintains the arc as we come to the hitting area, the left elbow becomes responsible for squaring up the clubface. The hands have nothing to do with it.

But how does the left elbow square up the clubface?

Notice the clubface in the photo on the left on page 150: the leading edge is *parallel* to the intended line of flight. Then notice the photo on the right: the leading edge of the clubface is *square* or *perpendicular* to the line of flight. The left elbow turning inward, propelled by the turning torso and shoulders, guides the powerful right side into the impact zone and squares the clubface through the hitting area.

John told me that Hogan continuously stressed, "If you continue to keep the arms as close together as possible, the left

The left elbow before it turns inward.

The left elbow after it turns inward.

elbow will turn toward the left hip and automatically square up the clubface—*if* you train it properly."

The most effective way to train the left elbow—and all of our players' movements—is through repeated slow swing motions.

Hogan's students are well aware of the right elbow's function throughout the entire swing, but I have yet to see or hear anyone discuss the left elbow and its indispensible function on the downswing.

Many top players get into trouble off the tee because they cannot coordinate the left elbow movement through the impact area. Tiger Woods is the most noticeable example of occasional left elbow malfunction (mainly because he is the most noticed golfer playing today). When he is struggling with the driver, his left elbow doesn't turn in through the hitting area. It points down the line, leaving the clubface open, causing pushes to the right of his target and a higher than normal finish.

Chances of this occurring are magnified in Tiger's swing because he has a tremendous turning motion, and centrifugal energy flows from his spinning body at a much higher speed than most golfers. I believe that if he worked more on training his left arm to turn inward through the impact area, he would be much more accurate off the tee.

You will be much more accurate off the tee, and with all your shots, if you train your left elbow to perform this important role in your swing.

You must rotate the club with your left arm *by turning your left elbow toward your hip.*

—Hogan to John Schlee

Downswing Phase 3— Capturing the Ball

Continue to turn the body until the clubface captures the ball.

Notice what is happening in the downswing from Phase 2 to Phase 3. The left hip has continued to turn, clearing a path for the hands to travel unrestricted. The weight is moving to the

Downswing phase 3—capturing the ball.

outside of the left foot. The shoulders continue to turn *around* the head.

The left elbow turns inward toward the left hip and squares the clubface. This allows the powerful right side to explode freely through the hitting area and *capture* the ball, as Hogan describes it. This is why Hogan wished he had the power of "three right hands."

When Hogan began to understand the workings of a repeatable golf swing, he realized that all his energy should not be directed toward a violent encounter with the ball. Instead, he envisioned his clubface capturing the ball and slinging it to the target. Thus the downswing energy is released toward the target and not at the ball. I believe this is what created a unique sound to Hogan's golf shots as he connected with the ball.

Remember, the left hand and left side guide the powerful right hand and right side to capturing the ball. Practice this motion slowly at first. The more comfortable you become, the faster you can go.

Checkpoints for Phase 3

1. Left side is totally cleared out of the way.
2. Weight is on the outside of the left foot.
3. Left elbow has turned in toward the left hip.
4. The palm of the right hand is moving toward the ground.
5. Head remains steady.

DETAILS OF THE IMPACT ZONE

By training the arms to stay close together, they will follow the turning body in a perfect semicircular orbit around the torso throughout the impact zone. In fact, with the left elbow turning inward near and through the impact zone, thearms *must* follow a perfect semicircle. The finishing movement will stay on a plane around the body and will not come up into a high finish. Justin Leonard and Jose Maria Olazabal are good examples of this inside-to-inside move.

As the hands orbit on plane into the impact zone, they pass over the right knee.

Now in Phase 3 of the downswing, the hands are passing over the left knee—not down the target line—on their orbit around the torso.

These photos show the arms and the hands following a precise semicircular movement from inside to inside along the swing plane. With the left elbow turned inward, the clubface will be square as it meets the ball.

Impact Zone Checklist

One of John's favorite playing pals, Sam Snead, had this to say: "Good positions do not produce good swings. A good swing produces good positions with lots of motion." Hogan said essentially the same thing in his *Five Lessons*.

Lock this into your mind: positions do not create motions; motions create positions. Our entire focus is on making the right movements, which naturally will move all of our body parts through the right places at the right times.

Here's a checklist of right places to be as the club passes through the ball:

- **Left knee remains flexed.** One of the more damaging movements in the impact zone is to straighten out the left leg. This happens when the weight isn't allowed to transfer to the outside of the left foot—and that is usually caused by the hands leading, rather than following, the arms.

  John said that Hogan was adamant about keeping the left knee flexed through impact. Hogan knew that if you straightened the left leg, it would prohibit the hip turn, stop or reverse the weight flow, and restrict the surge of energy into the hitting area. This also opens up a Pandora's box of golf swing miscues.

  Picture this: A golfer straightens his left leg through impact, which raises his body and causes him to top the ball. His mental micromanager gets to work and says, "Maybe if I uncock my wrists a little early, I can at least hit the ball." He tries another shot and releases his wrists sooner, losing power in the process, and hits it fat. His micromanager then says, "I must be too close to the ball, so let's back away a little," and on and on.

You see where I'm going. Too many times, we respond to a poor shot by trying to quick-fix a bad diagnosis. Don't be misled by effects. Go back to the fundamentals and find the causes. In this case, as you can see, the cause of the mishaps is straightening the left leg. Correct that, and you automatically eliminate the unwanted aftereffects.

- **Head is directly over or slightly behind the ball.** This is where your head will be if you start your downswing by turning the hips and letting shoulders, arms, and hands follow in orbit around your torso.

- **Right elbow is pointed down and kept close in to the torso.** This anchors the downswing movement and keeps it on plane.

- **Left elbow is turned inward.** This move squares the clubface at impact and keeps arms working as a single coordinated unit.

- **Hands follow the arm movements.** Relaxed hands are released for their final snap through the ball.

John gave his students a couple tips on getting a feeling for the hands heading into the impact area. "Pretend you are a waiter carrying a tray full of dishes. When you start your downswing, take the tray, turn it over, and smash it to the ground as your body turns toward the hitting area. Don't forget to keep the right elbow pointed to the ground."

Don't worry, your right palm won't continue going straight down. What begins at the top as a downward movement with the right palm quickly becomes a sideways movement into the ball as you turn and the right hand pivots around the right elbow.

John's illustration always got mixed reactions. When we walked students through this motion, many were astonished at how natural it felt.

John also described it as a wiping motion: "When your right hand goes through impact, I want you to feel as though you are wiping the ground with the palm of your right hand [right to left motion]." In both illustrations, imagine the wrist and heel pad of your right hand leading into the impact area. This will be its position if the right wrist remains cocked, as it should, until just *after* impact.

The palm up at the top of the swing.

The palm side down, approaching impact.

The palm "wiping" through impact.

The palm continues toward the target.

THE FOLLOW-THROUGH

Hogan showed me how the left elbow folds on the way through just as the right elbow folds on the way back.

—*John Schlee*

The Follow-Through—The Extension

The beginning of the follow-through is the continuation of the turn until the right arm is parallel to the ground and the left elbow points to the ground.

Our lower body and upper body are moving so fast at this point we have no control unless our players have been trained in what

The arms remain close together through the finish.

path to take. Here again, we address the need for the lower body to keep moving. We also look at our arms to make sure they are still as close together as possible.

This close connection of the arms in the follow-through creates a mirror image to the backswing. The left elbow folds and points to the ground on the follow-through, as the right elbow folded and pointed to the ground on the backswing.

Watch this movement in slow motion, and gain confidence in your ability to repeat this motion.

It is important to understand that we must train these parts of the body to carry out their duties accurately even after the ball has left the clubface. They must know where they are going, or they can hinder the turn and misdirect the shot.

So don't take the follow-through for granted. Repeat this movement over and over until your body instinctively knows where to go.

Checkpoints for the Follow-Through

1. More weight moves to the outside of the left foot.
2. Hips are facing the target.
3. Left elbow is pointing toward the ground.
4. Right arm is extended.
5. Right shoulder is under the chin.

You can never be a good long driver of the golf ball until you allow your hands to "fly" by your left ear on the finish of the swing.

—*John Schlee*

The Follow-Through—The Finish

The finish is a continuation of the turn into the follow-through until the right shoulder points to the target.

You have finally come to the conclusion of your golf swing. This final element of the follow-through is best understood as a reaction to the entire swing before it. Now is the time to find out how you did.

Release momentum flies you to the finish.

Checkpoint Questions for the Follow-Through

1. Is your completed finish well balanced?
2. Is your right shoulder over your left toe?
3. Is your left knee still flexed?
4. Is the weight on the outside of the left foot toward the heel?

If you answer no to any of these questions, you must investigate where the breakdown occurred. The more you practice the movements in each swing phase, the easier it will be to discover where any lapses occur in the sequence of the swing.

As Hogan would say, the finish of your golf swing will tell you how well you performed the sequence of movements he termed the *chain action*. When you follow the proper sequence from the top of the swing (starting with your knees and hips, shoulders, arms, and then hands) through the impact zone, the finish will reflect positive results every time. If your arms and hands remain relaxed and supple, they will indeed "fly" all the way around and past your left ear, as John recommends.

So at first, concentrate on learning the motions properly, and don't let the outcome of the shot totally dictate your review of the swing. I'm sure you've heard the saying "a blind squirrel finds an acorn every now and then." Only the right movements in an orderly sequence can make your supply of acorns reliable and plentiful.

○ ○ ○

Keep an eye on your "players" to make sure each one is performing properly. Continue to practice and study each motion in detail until all of your players learn their jobs and work together as a tightly knit team. I've set up the following practice guide as a quick and easy way for you to find success with this swing system.

Remember, you are the coach, the one in charge of this whole operation. Your players will do what you train them to do. I wish you a long run of winning seasons.

What Next? Practice, of Course

In a short time, you can incorporate the Legendary Golf swing into your game if you follow a regular practice routine. I recommend starting with four 20-minute sessions a week for four weeks. I've outlined a general training guide (as follows) that you can easily adapt to suit your goals.

As with anything, your progress will be a direct reflection of your focus and commitment to learning.

Stick to this schedule, and within thirty days, these swing movements should feel natural and comfortable. Continue for another thirty days, and the movements should be almost ingrained. By that time, you will be moving through the swing phases with more emphasis on their feel and with less thinking about details.

As you continue, customize your practice schedule to work on any challenging areas, using the slow-motion movements as your guide. It's a good idea to conduct an occasional review and walk yourself through all the swing phases. Here's an easy, effective practice plan.

The First Two Weeks at Home

I recommend going through each setup and swing phase in slow motion during your twenty-minute sessions for the first two weeks. Begin each session with a few minutes of gentle stretching.

Do *not* go to the practice range during the first two weeks because you will naturally become "ball oriented." If you start hitting balls before you are prepared, you will likely be influenced too much by the result of each ball hit. You will tend to revert to old swing habits because they will still seem more familiar and comfortable.

So forget the ball for a while. Let this be your "incubator" time, where pure swing training is the top priority.

The Next Two Weeks at Home and on the Range

As you continue your weekly home sessions, gradually work into hitting balls on the practice range. Start with one range session per week. The following are important tips for the practice range:

- Take several practice swings before each shot, carefully monitoring the performance of your "team players" through the setup and swing phases.
- Begin with at least ten *half* swings as you begin to hit balls. Half swings will help you develop timing and tempo. Until

you can hit a ball properly going half speed, there is no need to try your swing at full speed.

- Move on to full swings when you feel ready. Monitor your swing carefully to make sure your players are performing properly in each phase. Again, don't be too concerned with ball performance at this point.

- Pay attention to your finish because it is a gauge of the development of your entire swing.

Remember, practice takes work that only you can perform. You are the coach, and only consistent training can get your team working as one powerhouse unit. You now hold all the keys to building and developing a sound golf swing. It's up to you to continue the work and enjoy the fruits of your labor for years to come.

On the Golf Course

When you feel ready, go out and try your new swing on the golf course. I'm sure you know that practicing your swing is quite different from playing the game.

John Schlee told me that when you are making a swing change, use it on the practice tee, but play with your old swing on the golf course. John said that Hogan reminded him that you need your total mental focus when playing. He said you can't stay focused on your targets if you're preoccupied with keeping track of swing movements.

That may seem like tricky advice, but there's some wisdom to it. During your transition, you probably will try your new swing on the course but will end up playing with your old one for a while. A melding process will take place gradually as you gain enough confidence in your new swing to start using it on the golf course. You will know when the time is right to switch over and commit to your new swing.

I wish you the best on your adventure into the world of Legendary Golf. If you have any questions or complaints or just want to talk about anything in this book, please get in touch. I'd be happy to visit with you.

Tom Bertrand
The Legendary Golf System
P.O. Box 3673
Vista, CA 92085
golfersrgr8@yahoo.com
www.thesecretofhogansswing.com

Acknowledgments

Legends of our heroes are often more embellished by speculation than by real information, but in the case of the legendary Ben Hogan, the golfing world is fortunate in having two biographers whose research and writing skills offer us a wealth of documented facts on his life and times. Curt Sampson's *Hogan* (1997) is the first major biography to chronicle details of Hogan's life and career, with a clear accounting of his early struggles, his rise to prominence, the fateful car accident, and an excellent summary of his record. James Dodson later wrote his monumental *Ben Hogan: An American Life* (2004). With access to family records and the cooperation of Hogan's wife, Valerie, Dodson compiled what is considered a definitive work on Hogan, the man and the era. We made extensive use of these biographies for background information in the chapter titled "Tracking the Secret."

Thanks to *Golf Digest* for permission to quote from their storehouse of Hogan material. We have supplemented our training section with quotations from Hogan's classic *Five Lessons: The Modern Fundamentals of Golf*, the bible of golf instruction and a must-read for every golfer. Other quoted sources include

John Schlee's *Maximum Golf* (book and video) and John Andrisani's *The Hogan Way.*

For additional perspective, we appreciate the fine sports journalism of Bill Fields, whose thoughtful feature piece on John Schlee appeared in *Golf World* magazine.

Special thanks to author and matey Steven Pressfield for being his naturally generous self, a fountain of inspiration and guidance from conception to completion of this work. We also thank one of the best golf writers in the business today, Jaime Diaz of *Golf Digest*, for kindly listening and encouraging this couple of nobodies back when we started this project.

In the business of book publishing, it is a relief to know that a person of the highest integrity, expertise, and goodwill is looking out for you, which is what literary agent Bob Diforio has been doing for us—thanks, Bob, for being the best. Thanks also to one of the last of the great gentlemen in the business, Larry Hughes, for his special help along the way. We also thank our editor, Stephen S. Power, for bringing us through the gate at John Wiley & Sons, a venerable publishing house with whom we're honored to be listed.

We appreciate the many people who shared their memories of the Maximum Golf School era: former teaching partners Gregg Graham, Lin Wicks, and Bruce Petz; John Schlee's former wife, Gay; plus the masters of their trades, Danny Ashcraft and Bob Vokey.

Many thanks to the fine folks at the Carlsbad City Library, who provided exceptional service in helping us search through their well-stocked periodicals section, and to Sara MacCalman, for ferreting out typos and word usage anomalies in the manuscript.

For patiently enduring our long withdrawals from normal

cognition, especially during the final weeks of finishing this manuscript, we thank the heavens for our wonderful soulmates, Heidi Bertrand and Kim Lugthart. Not only have they stretched their tolerance for "guys and their golf thing" beyond our expectations, these angels encouraged and nursed us along as only the best of friends do.